Harnessing the Power of Grief

Julie Potter, MSW, LCSW

Copyright 2020 by MSI Press LLC

All rights reserved. No part of this book may be reproduced or utilized in any form or by any means, electronic or mechanical, including photocopying, recording, or by any information storage and retrieval system, without permission in writing from the publisher.

For information, contact

MSI Press, LLC
1760 Airline Hwy, #203
Hollister, CA 95023

Cover design: Carl D. Leaver

Cover image: ShutterStock/Azur13

Permission to use specific content from Center for Loss and Life Transition granted by Companion Press.

Permission to use specific content granted by Dr. Alan Wolfelt.

Library of Congress Control Number: 2019918954

ISBN: 978-1-950328-14-7

Table of Contents

List of Tables. v

Acknowledgments. vii

Introduction. 1

Part 1
GRIEF PAST AND PRESENT 11

Chapter 1 What Grief Is and Why It Is Important 13

Chapter 2 Grief in Modern Times 19

Chapter 3 The Experience of Grief
and What It Might be Like for You 31

Part 2
THE TASKS OF GRIEF: What you do to make it through 45

Chapter 4 Task 1: To Accept the Reality of the Loss 47

Chapter 5 Task 2: To Experience the Pain of Grief—
Experiencing the Pain of Anger and Fear 57

Chapter 6 Task 2: To Experience the Pain of Grief—
Experiencing the Pain of Guilt and Shame. 75

Chapter 7 Task 2: To Experience the Pain of Grief—
Experiencing the Pain of Sadness and Depression 87

Chapter 8 Task 2: To Experience the Pain of Grief—
Experiencing Spiritual Pain. 101

Chapter 9 Task 3: To Adjust to a World
without the Deceased 109

Chapter 10 Task 4: To Embark on a New Life
While Establishing a Place in Your Heart for
Your Deceased Loved One. 123

Part 3
SPECIAL CONSIDERATIONS 131
    Chapter 11 Sudden Death 133
    Chapter 12 Ambiguous Loss 151
    Chapter 13 Styles of Grieving 157

Part 4
GUIDES TO UNDERSTANDING 167
    Chapter 14 Grief Guide: Tips and Validations 169
    Chapter 15 Danger Guide: Danger Signs to Watch For 179
    Chapter 16 Help Guide: How to Help 183
    Chapter 17 Summing Up 189
    Bibliography 191

List of Tables

Table 5.1
Fears I am experiencing. Anger I am experiencing................ 64

Table 5.2
Fearful ruminations and the power of imagination................. 65

Table 5.3
Angry ruminations and the power of imagination 66

Table 6.1
The differences and similarities between guilt and shame 77

Table 7.1
Possible distinctions between normal grief
sadness and clinical depression 90

Table 13.1
Gender-related differences in relationships 164

Acknowledgments

Thank you to my husband Tom and my daughter Gail who encouraged me to write the book. You both are lights in my life.

Thank you to the five readers: Tom Potter, Diane Brown, Barbara Compitello, Denise Mercier, and Lorraine Schmidt. Thank you for your encouragement and love in addition to your wording and grammar ideas.

Thank you to Widowed Persons Outreach (WPO), and its sponsoring community organizations, including my former employer Sibley Memorial Hospital. WPO volunteers help newly bereaved spouses on their journey through grief. I had the privilege to work with you for 20 years as the Coordinator of WPO. Many of you contributed stories to this book, and your stories will help many people. As we always reminded ourselves: when you help someone, you yourself are helped. Thank you, Widowed Persons Outreach, for helping me. It was my work with you that taught me that there is not one way to grieve: there is your way to grieve.

Thank you to the Library of Congress staff. I spent many hours there. Everyone there was helpful: the librarians, the staff who work behind the desk, cafeteria personnel. When I would get lost—it's a big place—people would notice the disoriented look on my face and reach out to help.

Thank you to the many people who have devoted their lives to helping people in grief, doing research on this subject, and writing about it. I may never meet you in person, but your work inspired me to continue writing.

Thank you to my ancestors and my fellow travelers. We are all together in this human and planetary journey. And grief is a big part of that journey.

Introduction

Grief, the process by which we adjust to the losses in our lives, is often one of the most devastating and life-changing experiences in a human being's life. Like all who have come before us, each of us will suffer important losses and will experience grief. A fraction of us will experience complicated grief and will benefit from professional help. Treatment of complicated grief is beyond the scope of this book, as discussed below. Most of us will experience normal grief, still very difficult, but manageable without professional help. In time, with our inner and outer resources, we will make a satisfactory adjustment to our loss. How do we do this? We harness the power of grief, and that is the subject of this book.

In my career, I coordinated a hospital-based wellness program including a spousal bereavement program. Volunteers, who themselves had been widowed for at least two years, provided help and support to those who were newly widowed. The volunteers attended monthly meetings to talk about those whom they were helping and to learn more about the subject of grief.

At each volunteer meeting, my team leader and I led discussions on various topics, based on the newest studies on grief and traditional knowledge about grief. A recognized expert would publish an article that we would discuss. A new book would come out, and we would review it together. There would be an article in the paper. Someone would bring in her favorite grief book. Therapists would be invited to give lectures. My team leader and I would present topics on grief. Rarely did everyone agree entirely with what was presented, and we would often hear: "It wasn't like that for me;" "I think you are missing an important point;" and "I agree with this, but not with that." The discussions were always lively.

We came away with the appreciation that each one of us is different. Even though there is a lot of research-based knowledge as well as traditional knowledge on the subject, each grief experience is unique. There is not one way to grieve. There are *your* ways to grieve. Knowledge supports you in your inner journey, but you are the one who writes the story.

Yet, knowledge has an important place. Knowledge gives you a framework for your journey. Knowledge gives you hope. Others have walked this path, and you can, too. Knowledge validates your experience and gives you confidence. Duane T. Bowers (2006), a counselor in Washington, DC, reminds us, "Grief will happen—don't worry, it will happen. Many people think it is not happening or that if it is happening, they are doing it wrong. The problem arises when people get anxious and stressed about it" (n.p.). He encourages us to relax. Grief happens naturally and differently for each person.

George A. Bonanno, a well-known clinical psychologist, author and grief researcher, speaks about grief this way: "Above all, it [grief] is a human experience. It is something we are wired for, and it is certainly not meant to overwhelm us. Rather, our reactions to grief seem designed to help us accept and accommodate losses relatively quickly so that we can continue to live productive lives" (2009, p. 7). "Relatively quickly" is different for each person: a few months, one year, two years, six years....

Throughout the rest of your life, your grief may return, albeit not necessarily with the same intensity. At first, these returns may be frequent, scary, and painful. With time, these returns become less frequent and probably less intense. They are a connection to your loved one. They are a connection to others who also have experienced losses. Grief and its returns are a connection to humankind. Even though we may feel alone, we are together.

Much of the body of valuable research on grief goes back decades, even to the days of Sigmund Freud. The more recent research is refining but not revolutionizing the work of the past. Studies of the grief traditions of different cultures, including cultures that are thousands of years old, have also contributed to our present-day understanding of grief and its powerful place in the collective life of humankind.

Although knowledge continues to evolve through research, William Worden, clinical psychologist and researcher, suggests that we do not have to create a new theory of grief. Instead, we need to refine what the past 100 years of grief knowledge and study have brought forth. You will consequently note that there are new references that continue to validate much of the older work. As Worden (2015) says,

> Looking at the various theories of grief that have been proffered over the past 100 years is a bit like the fable of the blind men and the elephant. The description of what the elephant was like depended on what part of the elephant the various blind men were touching. Grief theory makes up the elephant—conceptions of the adaptation to the loss of a loved one with their various similarities and differences. However, the elephant needs a pedicure! Rather than recreating the elephant, we need to select and investigate specific parts of these theories (toes) and tweak them (p. 98).

In 1982, Worden himself introduced the idea of the four Tasks of Grief, an idea that continues to have merit today. Part 2 of this book is devoted to Worden's Tasks.

What this book includes:

In Part 1, "Grief Past and Present," I define grief as a natural human response to loss, the way we incorporate the loss into our lives and then move on in life. I trace the individual and community history of grief in Western culture from the rural small-town past to modern times. By looking at the past, we gain a fuller appreciation of how we are experiencing grief in this present day and age. As Joe Piehuta, an old family friend, put it, "If you don't know where you are, you don't know who you are." This look at the past helps us in the present. It gives us power in the present.

We will see how our transient, individualistic, and modern society presents challenges for the grieving person who does not always receive adequate support from his community. We can learn from our past, and we can learn from other cultures. Other cultures see death and grief as the natural progression of human existence, not as an aberration and an affront to one's sensibilities.

We will explore the experience of grief and what it might be like for you. Our modern culture does not have a unified view of grief so you may feel blindsided by the experience. Consequently, it is helpful for you to know what you might experience in grief: a loss of meaning; judgment of yourself and others; a changed view of the world and your place in it; the oscillation between your grief experience and navigating in a changed world; middle knowledge (one moment you know the death has occurred, and the next moment you don't); and the presence of reminders that trigger grief reactions. Exploring the many ways grief may manifest helps you to accept what you are experiencing as normal and to accept the experience of others.

In Part 2, "The Tasks of Grief," I use William Worden's Tasks of Grief as the framework for our discussion of grieving. Other authors use stages of grief, which imply that if you go through one stage, you are ready for the next. When you complete all the stages, you are finished. Then, you move on. Yet, many researchers have found that grief does not follow a timeline from beginning to end. Grief is a dynamic process, and we never completely "get over it." As human beings, we will find grief always to be a part of our lives. With the passage of time, our relationship with the deceased and our memories become deeper or take on new facets as we ourselves change and grow. The Tasks of Grief can continue throughout your life.

The tasks summarize the process of grief—what you do to make it through:

Task 1. To accept the reality of the loss (Chapter 4)

Task 2. To experience the pain of grief (Chapters 5 through 8)

Task 3. To adjust to a world without the deceased (Chapter 9)

Task 4. To embark on a new life while establishing a place in your heart for your deceased loved one (Chapter 10)

The tasks honor the uniqueness of each grief experience. You can work on the tasks in order, in any order, or all at once. You may find it helpful to revisit each or all the tasks at different times throughout your life. Working with the tasks, completing the task(s), and revisiting the tasks are ways to harness the power of grief.

Some tasks may be easy for you to complete. Others, not so easy.

The Tasks of Grief describe a powerful process in which you are in charge (although you may not always feel that way). These imply action rather than passive experience. As will be described in Chapter 2, when people do something, they feel better. The tasks honor the complexity of the grief process by recognizing the variety of ways individuals accomplish things and the effort needed to do so. There is room for individual variation in how much or how little and what kinds of attention you choose to give to each task. To harness the power of the tasks, see them as a creative process and a labor of love for your loved one, yourself, your family, and your community.

When a loved one dies, your sense of meaning can be changed, challenged, deepened, damaged, and even shattered. Within each task is the search for meaning: finding meaning in the loss, finding meaning in the pain, finding meaning in your loved one's life and death, finding meaning in your own life, and reaffirming and/or rebuilding a meaningful life.

The tasks can be perennial. At times throughout your life, you may be inclined to revisit the tasks. Often this occurs because you have acquired new knowledge. After a time, you may feel complete with your grief process, but then years later, something will happen that will rekindle thoughts of the deceased in a new way—an event or a new bit of knowledge (positive or negative) that will give you a different look at the past and your relationship with the deceased.

A reminder may pop up in your consciousness, bringing up a loss from long ago. New meaning in your life and in your memories of the deceased may evolve. John Jordan (2015), a clinical psychologist specializing in grief and bereavement says, "Grief is a cyclical revisiting process" (n.p.). He suggests that you imagine that you are going up a spiral staircase. As you go up, you make a full circle and return to your beginning point but on a higher or different level. At each return, you have the opportunity and maybe the inclination to see things in a different light and from a different perspective. At each return, you are different, your world is different, and new insights can unfold. You may be inspired to revisit one or more of the tasks, to accept the loss and to appreciate the life of your loved one in a different, a more nuanced, and maybe a deeper way.

New losses bring up old losses. When you experience a loss, you may revisit previous losses, or shall I say, they re-visit you. It may seem for a time that they come back to you with painful intensity. You may revisit one or all the tasks, and once again reaffirm or re-create your sense of meaning in your life.

Special events may rekindle your grief—weddings, graduations, funerals of others who died at the same age or in the same way as your loved one, family reunions, and birthdays. Children whose parent has died may miss that parent at each growth milestone and special event—a first day at school, a graduation, a marriage, or the birth of a child. Parents whose child has died may mourn what could have been at those same events and milestones: "This could have been my son's first day at school" or "If my son were alive, he would be graduating today."

Everyday experiences may rekindle your grief and inspire you to revisit one or more of the tasks. When I had a severe case of the flu as an adult, suddenly the thought came to me, "I wish my mother were alive. She really knew how to take care of me when I was sick." I reminisced about all those common yet unpleasant childhood illnesses and how she was there for me. I did not experience an intense grief experience; rather it was a gentle love, appreciation, and gratitude.

In keeping with the philosophy of the tasks, please feel free to read the task chapters in order or according to your interest or to what you are experiencing.

In my years of bereavement work, thinking of the grief process within the framework of these tasks seemed to make the most sense. However, I have found merit in many of the other authors' paradigms. Their insights can be readily incorporated into the Tasks of Grief framework. I have noted their work throughout this book (Bowers, Jordan, Doka and Martin, Golden, Duggan, Bowen, Parkes, Rando, Stroebe, Bonanno, Westberg, Yeagley, Kübler-Ross, Weissman, Rynearson, Ochberg, Leedy). Their work does not negate the tasks. Instead, they complement and add depth to them. Please refer to the bibliography for information about these and other authors.

In his book, *Grief Recovery*, Reverend Larry Yeagley (1984) briefly describes four broad steps to work through the grief process: Think. Write. Talk. Weep. I have adapted Yeagley's work for this book, using his four steps as a springboard to develop a number of practices, each tailored to particular grief tasks and other particular conditions. I do not refer to these practices as steps, as he does. To me a step seems to say that once you complete the step, you are finished with it. Rather the practices and the tasks are here for you to use repeatedly and comfortably.

In Part 3, "Special Considerations," we explore two specific kinds of losses: sudden death and ambiguous loss. When your loved one dies suddenly, there is no time to prepare and no chance for you to say goodbye. One minute she is here, the next minute she is gone. On the other hand, an ambiguous loss is one that does not end and continues to evolve. Your loved one may have Alzheimer's disease with many losses of functioning long before the actual death occurs. Or your loved one is Missing in Action. Although the evidence points to her death, there still is the small chance that she is alive.

We will also look at different styles of grieving. Some people prefer the company of others in their grief. Others seek solitude. Some people grieve in an emotional or feeling way, others in a thought-oriented way. Your grief history, your age, your sexual orientation, and the type of loss all influence your grieving.

Part 4, "Guides to Understanding," gives you a quick pick-me-up (Chapter 14, "Tips and Validations") when you don't feel like reading a chapter or even reading much at all but would just like some reassurance. It is there for those times when you are particularly affected by your grief and may be wondering if you need extra help (Chapter 15, "Danger Signs"). It is there, too, for the helper (Chapter 16, "How to Help"). All of us will at one time or another have the opportunity and the privilege to be a helper. As a grieving person, your first job is to help yourself and to come to a more comfortable place in your own life. However, as time goes on, you may want to reach out and help others who have experienced a loss. On the other hand, as a newly grieving person you may want to share Chapter 16 with those helpful family and friends who may clumsily be trying to offer help but do not know what to do. (Most of us have been in that position many times in our lives).

This book is filled with common-sense ideas. A person's confidence in exercising common sense in managing his grief is likely to be challenged during the grieving process. The common-sense ideas are the ones that help to open the door of hope and give you access to your inner power. They may also simply validate what you might be doing already, thereby increasing your power.

Grief is natural to humans. If you are a person, you will grieve. With every change, positive or negative, big or small, there is loss, and thus there is grief. We greet what is new, and we miss what we had. We incorporate our rich history and experience into our present life.

Death is the final event, the one from which there is no return. This book focuses on death, yet the information herein can be applied to all kinds of losses.

What this book is not:

You will not find case histories of individuals and families. Rather, you will find anecdotes of grieving people who have been willing to share their important moments with you. I believe that case histories can actually stop you in your tracks: "That person's experience is worse than mine." "I shouldn't complain." Actually, I believe you should complain. Your experience is unique, and comparisons to others do not always help. Comparisons can diminish your power to grieve in your own way and to appreciate your own way of grieving.

I do not believe that we grieve in a case history kind of way. (Therapists, however, need to know your case history, current situation, family history and dynamics, work history, and the like in order to help). You as a grieving person are helping yourself, and you will experience pivotal moments that will reveal to you where you are going and how far you have come. It is not always helpful to get involved in the long and nuanced stories that are another's grief. It is better to focus on your own grief. The stories in this book are moments that are there to help you on your way.

This book is not about complicated grief, that is, intense and unremitting grief that benefits from, and may require, professional help. The words "complicated grief" only appear here in the introduction. However, I point the way toward professional help in the "When to get Help" sections included in most of the chapters with easy-to-read warning signs to watch for. Inclusion of comprehensive discussions of therapeutic interventions and research is not appropriate for this book because this is a book about normal grief. Nonetheless, the grieving process is difficult even for normal grief, and this book is intended to help.

How to read this book:

Grief is unique for each person. One person may struggle with sadness, another with anger, another with the loss of meaning, another with guilt, another with feelings associated with trauma, and another with loneliness. Refer to the chapters that suit you in the moment that you pick up the book.

Throughout the book, I suggest many practices to help you in your grief. Some may be helpful to you in some situations, but not in others. They may be helpful either individually or in combinations and at different points in time during your grief process. Try them out and find the ones that work for you. You will find that many of them simply come naturally to you. In that case, they are here to validate your experience.

I encourage you to use this book to work with your thoughts and feelings. Most of the chapters include recommendations and exercises that you can do. For example, it is good to talk about your experience, and what you are thinking and feeling, with trusted friends, family, your deceased loved one, and yourself (in the form of journaling or creative expression). This idea of talking is repeated, reinforced, and discussed in different ways throughout the book. Some other examples are physical exercise, music, poetry, relaxation techniques, and memorial ideas.

Read the table of contents for ideas of where to start, then go to that chapter. If you are overwhelmed and feel that every chapter applies to you, simply pick one. The amazing thing about working through grief is that if you are helped in one area, this will influence other areas in your grieving and in your life. It is like facing a daunting home maintenance project—like spring-cleaning. You start with one drawer in one dresser. You tidy it up and rearrange it. Afterward, you feel like you have accomplished an amazing amount and are inspired to continue just by carefully cleaning one drawer.

Although I know enough about grief to write about it, I do not know enough to write about your own unique experience of grief. That is your story to "write," your story to tell. If this book helps you to find your own answers, then I will have succeeded.

We may buy a cookbook with the intention of trying every recipe in the book, but the common experience is that we pick one, two, or three recipes—that is the extent of our use. Years later, we may return to the cookbook and try out another few recipes. In reading this book, you may find that one chapter—maybe this one—one thought, one vignette, or one quote will resonate with you, and that will be enough. You may find a reference that takes you beyond what is written here and inspires you to go in a different direction. I encourage you to be on the lookout for your own favorite "recipe" and to change it up to suit your own experience.

My wish for you is that you find your own answers and come to appreciate your own inner power as you continue your journey of grief.

Julie Potter, MSW, LCSW

Part 1
GRIEF PAST AND PRESENT

This section includes an overview of grief: what grief is and why it is important, how grief was experienced in the past, how it is generally experienced today, and how you as an individual might experience it.

Julie Potter, MSW, LCSW

Chapter 1

What Grief Is and Why It Is Important

"We have all come through it, or we will all come to it."
—Elizabeth Alexander[1]

Grief is a natural human response.

Most of us can adjust and adapt to life's daily changes and losses. We have goals in mind, and we have an idea of how life is going to go. We have a level of comfort about our skills as each day proceeds. We rapidly adjust to the little changes of life—the traffic jam, the toddler's tantrum, the meeting that goes on and on, the unidentified noise in the night, the forgotten item at the grocery store.

Think of how many times in the day we have to take a deep breath, mutter some exasperated words, say a prayer, try to be patient and loving, or try to be strong in the face of our goals and dreams being thwarted or challenged by life's little changes. Loss is present but not overwhelming, and we easily manage to do what we must to stay on track.

As the changes get bigger, the stakes get higher. Loss then becomes a more apparent and more strongly felt companion to change. Even with positive changes—the ones we sign up for—we still lose something. We marry and lose the freedom of single life. We get a job and lose our dependence on Mom and Dad. Our child grows up, and now our house is empty. We grow old and face the loss of loved ones, our jobs, physical and mental capabilities, even the shared rich history of by-gone times. We say

---
1   This quote comes from an interview with Alexander (2015) in the *PBS NewHour*.

hello to what is, and we miss what was. It is not always easy to make this reconciliation between what is and what was. With each change, we acquire a changed identity, sometimes very quickly, sometimes slowly. We become a spouse, an employee, a parent, an older person. We grow into our changed identities, and we may miss our old ones, too.

Then, there are the changes that we do not sign up for. These losses can affect us deeply. When loved ones change or die or when our meaningful activities change or end, we may feel that a part of us changes or dies, too. A dream is shattered. We may feel betrayed. It is not only the direct loss. It is the loss of who we are or who we think we are. By far, the death of a loved one is the most poignant and challenging loss.

How do we make it through life's losses and broken dreams? How do we figure out who we are afterward? How do we incorporate these losses, many of them tragic, and move on in life with renewed love and joy? How do we find meaning in our life after we experience a loss? How do we remember?

Grieving is the way. When we experience the pain of grief, we may think that these emotions are negative. We want to get over them, get through them, and get relief from them. Peter McWilliams, author of *You Can't Afford the Luxury of a Negative Thought*, tells us that as painful as these feelings are, they are a natural human response to loss: "...mourning is a positive human activity. It allows us the flexibility to adapt to change. It is not 'negative' to feel pain, fear, and anger at a loss. It's a natural human response" (1995, p. 123).

If grief is natural to us, then why do we need a book about it? Because we do not have a generally supportive culture to lead the way and pave a way for us in grief. Grief is still seen as a short-term disturbance. We grieve, but we also feel that we have to live as if everything is normal. But it is not. Everything has changed or has completely fallen apart, and now we think we must figure it all out for ourselves.

Grief is love.

Barbara J. King, anthropologist and author, tells us that there is evidence that prehistoric human beings buried their dead carefully and lovingly. Special tokens were buried with the deceased. The care taken suggests that the survivors loved those who died. In Russia, archeologists discovered two bodies of young children that were over 24,000 years old. Many carvings and husks surrounded them, and hundreds of hand-made ivory beads were sewn into their clothing (King, 2013). The evidence suggests that the children were loved and that those who loved them grieved their loss.

Marc Bekoff, Professor Emeritus of Ecology and Evolutionary Biology at the University of Colorado has studied animals in nature, and from his observations, believes that grief seems to occur in animals. When a mammal in the wild dies, others in the herd, sometimes at risk to themselves, will hover around the body and appear to offer comfort to one another. The surviving mammals, particularly those in close love relationships, like a mate or a parent, appear to be despondent. If an animal disappears from the herd, adults and cubs may search for the missing animal (Bekoff, 2007).

Love and grief are intertwined. Gerald May, MD, a psychiatrist and, until his death, Senior Fellow in Contemplative Theology and Psychology at the Shalem Institute in Washington, DC, said, "Although it seldom feels like it, grief is an authentic expression of love" (1992, p. 3). Each of us in the privacy of our hearts knows when we have loved authentically. We are heart-to-heart. We remember those moments for the rest of our lives. In those moments of grief, we know, even though it may be painful, that we are connecting with our deceased loved one in a way that does not ask—because it cannot—for a return of love. Grief is an expression of love for that which is gone.

Grief makes the loss real.

A common statement from someone who is newly bereaved is, "I can't believe it." You may even behave at times as if the deceased is still alive—setting a place for him at the table or calling him on the phone. Then, once again the realization of the loss dawns. Grief helps you to accept the reality of the loss.

The funeral events and services bring home the reality. Yes, this did happen, and others in my community know it has happened, too.

The loss becomes real through memorial rituals, the recognition of anniversary events such as holidays and birthdays, telling the story over and over, and most poignantly, in experiencing the silence of absence.

Grief is unique for each loss.

Over your lifetime, you will experience many different losses and may even feel you are accustomed to loss. Yet you may be taken aback by your reactions. One loss will bring up tumultuous thoughts and feelings. Another loss you may take in stride and feel very little sadness. It can also take some time for the survivor to realize that she is affected by the loss.

Singer-songwriter Graham Lindsay sings, "We're all in this together alone." You are alone in that your grief is unique to you. Your relationship with your loved one was unique. Maybe others also had a relationship with your loved one, but it was a different relationship. When someone says, "I understand," "I've been there," or "Me, too," they haven't. No one can really understand what another person is experiencing. We can only listen to each other with love. In the documentary, *Stories We Tell*, Canadian writer and director, Sarah Polley, whose mother died when she was 11 years old, interviews significant people in her deceased mother's life to discover their narratives. Each person—siblings, spouse, friends, and a lover—had a different experience and different feelings about who Sarah's mother was and their relationship with her. And each experience was true for that person (Polley, 2012).

Grief will happen; you don't have to force it.

In my work with newly bereaved spouses, common first questions were, "Am I doing this right?" "One moment I don't know how I will make it. And another moment, I am happy. How can this be?" "Is there an end to this?"

You may wonder if grief is happening, if you are stuck, or if you even are doing it "right." Don't worry. Grief is a normal process, and grief will happen. Whether you are a griever or a helper, trust that grief is happening.

Grief helps you to discover a new you.

As confusing and painful as it may feel, grief helps you to discover new parts of yourself. Does this mean that you leave your loved one behind? Not at all. Before she died, according to Elaine Raue, Nancy Newkirk comforted her best friend by saying "Every person you have known is a part of who you are" (personal communication, April 5, 1998). Each person is a part of the rich tapestry of your life.

The death of your loved one halts your life's journey and changes your experience of living and functioning in the world. By necessity, you must learn new skills and perhaps take over activities that were once done by your loved one. Thus, your journey of grief is also a journey of discovery. You discover strengths and attributes about yourself that you may not have appreciated before.

Occasionally people get stuck in their grieving.

By and large, people make it through their grief and continue their lives. There are times when it may be hard for you, maybe too hard. There is help out there, and throughout the book I have noted signs for you to watch for to help you decide when to reach out for help.

Chapter Summary

Grief is a natural human response to loss. It is an expression of love. It helps you to make the loss real. It helps you to create a new you and to incorporate the memory of your loved one into your life. It helps you to move on with your life.

You may wonder if you are the exception. Earlier, I mentioned life's little changes. Contemplate the way you adjust to small changes and get back on track. The seeds are there for how you will adjust to the bigger changes and losses. You are coming into grief with your eyes open and are ready to do all that you can.

Julie Potter, MSW, LCSW

Chapter 2

Grief in Modern Times

"Are we perhaps simply formalizing and making applicable to urban life a procedure that would naturally be followed in rural and more closely knit communities?"
—*Phyllis Silverman*[2]

Where we are today

Western culture gives limited attention and support to those who are grieving. After a few weeks of grieving, our action-oriented culture thinks (and hopes) you are okay and wants you to return to normal. Some may seem uncomfortable in speaking with you. You may sense that people are avoiding you or avoiding the topic of your loss in conversation. The level of discomfort may increase with the severity of the loss, e.g., a homicide, a suicide, the death of a child, or a sudden death. People may also underestimate the effect on you of other kinds of losses: divorce, relocation, or retirement, and sooner than not, may lightheartedly say, "Congratulations!"

Public acknowledgement of death focuses on the funeral arrangements, including the funeral home viewing and service and perhaps an additional memorial service. Employers may give 2-5 days for bereavement leave. At a time when most vulnerable, the survivor faces additional time-consuming and stressful responsibilities beyond the funeral itself: notifying family and friends; administrative responsibilities, such as pro-

---

[2] Phyllis Silverman (1969, p. 337) studied widowed and children's grief and the benefits of mutual support.

viding death certificates to businesses, insurance companies and financial institutions; dealing with the will and the estate; and facing the reality that there may be fewer financial resources available to live on.

Death is private.

In many cultures, including ours in the West, death is a private event. Notwithstanding sudden or traumatic death when death can occur anywhere, anytime, people generally die at home or in a health care setting.

If one's final hour is in a hospital, one may be moved to a private room for privacy considerations of the patient and family. Removing the body from the room upon death is carried out surreptitiously so as not to disturb others. The body will be covered, and by the way the cloth is draped, it will not be recognizable as a body. Death is invisible in the hospital.

Death is a medical event.

If one dies in a medical facility, the medical professionals oversee the care: monitoring vital signs, giving treatments, recording the time of death, and noting the medical cause of death. Sometimes, things happen so quickly in an emergency that your permission for treatment will be solicited with little or no time for discussion or for your input. If you would like to refuse further treatment for yourself or for your loved one, your wishes hopefully will be honored but not before the doctors and you discuss the implications of your decision. If they don't agree with you, you may need to sign a form stating that your actions are "Against Medical Advice."

Even if your loved one dies at home, medical professionals become involved. You might dial 911 for assistance. If the death is expected, your first phone call will be to the doctor or to a medical agency overseeing the care such as a home health agency or hospice. After notifying the medical world, you would call family, your religious organization, and the funeral home. You might first call family or friends, but that would be to get advice. "This is what has happened. What should I do now? Who should I call?"

After the death, those in the medical profession necessarily move on to the next person's life to save, enhance, and treat. You have left the medical community and the team of doctors, nurses and various therapists who had been there by your side. You may receive condolence cards from them. They may even attend the funeral. After that, you may not hear from them again, and if you do, they may not have the time or inclination to talk with you about your loss. Many grieving people experience this as an additional loss.

Everyone does not know your loss because you belong to many separate communities.

In the city or town where you live, there may be many sub-communities and social networks. Those you work with may not know your family and friends. If you work for a big company, you may only know your department. Your neighbors may be different from your friends. You may have several friends or groups of friends who do not know one another. There may not be one overall umbrella community where you are known by everyone and where everyone knows and cares about you.

In our-present day Western culture, we do not have a ritual or a protocol that says to all the communities of which we are members, "I am grieving." You may look okay, but inside that may not be the case. This is one reason why people may feel alone and powerless in their grief.

Death is invisible for many years for a large segment of the population.

To survive to old age is common in modern society. You may not attend funerals regularly before the age of sixty. As a grieving person, you may be new to grief. Because others may also have little experience with grief and how to help a bereaved person, they may be uncomfortable around you, not knowing what to say or how to act. This may be less true in communities where racism, joblessness, violence, drugs, and poverty take too many lives, both young and old.

How we got here

From America's rural past in the 19th and early 20th centuries to the present, we have experienced sweeping changes in how we live, die, and grieve.

Grief in the 19th and early 20th centuries

Alan C. Swedlund, an anthropologist, studied village illness and death in Massachusetts in the 18th, 19th, and 20th centuries. Although his studies covered a small area, his insights appear to apply to the U.S. culture in general.

Prior to the 1850s, death was experienced as an event with family and close friends nearby. Death was private. Into the early 20th century, many illnesses were fatal, and their victims were primarily babies, children, and young adults. Scarlet fever, tuberculosis, whooping cough, diphtheria, typhoid fever, the flu, childbed fever, and pneumonia were common diagnoses. "Whereas each year in Massachusetts thousands of children died of infectious diseases, the numbers for those over sixty were in the hundreds" (Swedlund, 2010, p. 126).

There was little that could be done, except to make a diagnosis, help patients to be comfortable, and hope for the best. Doctors were scarce, and their methods were more folk medicine than science. My father, who grew up in a small town in New Hampshire during the early part of the 20th century, told me that when he was growing up, he would see young boys about his age sitting on their front porches, looking ill and tired. He knew that they were going to die of tuberculosis, the deadly disease of that time. We can be sure this was a sobering, frightening, and common occurrence. Death was a real and present possibility for most people.

Not that long ago, conditions that we see as serious but not necessarily life-threatening, such as compound fractures, could easily have resulted in an amputation and possibly death. The serious illnesses of today, cancer for one, were not experienced as often in the past probably because many people did not survive long enough to get them.

The medicalization of death

Little by little, with the advancement of medical knowledge, realistic hope for cures and for a long and productive life increased. The days of providing folk remedies and comfort care gave way to life-saving drugs and surgeries. Antibiotics, immunizations, and improved hygiene wiped out many lethal diseases. Children had a much greater chance to become adults. Young mothers and their babies could survive childbirth. Young adults could survive to old age.

Prior to 1850, artistic renderings of a person's final hour would include the minister. In later art, it was the doctor who was at the bedside (Swedlund, 2010). The medicalization of death had begun. Death became the intruder, a necessary evil to be forestalled and avoided, and at worst, a failure of medicine.

To look at grief today, we need to look at medicine. Medicine has removed the specter of death from daily life. No wonder we don't know how to act when someone dies. Medicine can even make us feel ashamed to die. One may refer to a loved one's death in this way: "He gave up the fight." There is a subtle undercurrent: "It is his fault that he died." "If he hadn't given up, maybe he would still be here today." "Maybe he shouldn't have given up." "I wish I had done more to encourage him to keep fighting." The recognition that there is a natural progression of life from birth to death has become a thing of the past.

Movement from the country to the city

At the same time medicine was working miracles and changing society's view of death, people were also migrating to cities in search of new lives and jobs. They left behind farm and village life where everyone knew each other.

A loss experienced in a village would be felt by all. If your loss was a death, everyone would know the person who died and would sympathize with you because they would have lost that person, too. Your loss affected the whole community. You may not have been on friendly terms with everyone, but everyone would know your loss. The loss could also be a house or barn burning down, loss of livestock, or a bad growing season that affected everyone's crops.

With migration to the city, a person left his community—an umbrella of safety and common knowledge—and became a member of multiple communities. Daily interactions now occurred with strangers—shopping, car upkeep, banking, dining, to name a few. Your loss would not be known by everyone.

What other cultures can teach us

Proximity to other cultures offers opportunities to adopt much of their wisdom into our own culture. Paul C. Rosenblatt, a psychologist, tells us that cultures are not static. They are in a state of change (some more than others) with many individual differences (Rosenblatt, 2008). A Buddhist, a Jewish person, an African American, a Protestant, will grieve in the unique ways of their cultures. Variations exist among subgroups (based on lifestyle and income, religious variations within and between denominations), intermarriage, and cross-cultural influences. Consequently, we all are bumping into one another, learning from one another, loving one another, reading about one another, and interacting with one another.

Funerals and memorial services in Western culture tend to stand alone, like shooting stars in the night. They may be memorable and beautiful, but then we are left with the rest of the night. In some cultures, funeral rites are part of the whole day of life: the setting sun, the coming of night, the dawn, and the new day. Here are some examples of what we can learn from other cultures.

Death is not a failure.

Many cultures do not see death as a failure or an aberration. Rather, death is regarded as a part of life to be experienced by everyone. Loss does not end at the occurrence of death and the funeral. The experience of the loss continues and changes in healthful and even joyful ways throughout one's life.

The Mexican holiday Día de los Muertos, Day of the Dead, is celebrated in the U.S. and other countries in Latin America. Everyone remembers the deceased in a festive way, with meals, social gatherings, church altars with pictures and mementos associated with the deceased, and processions to the cemetery. The activities and foods that are prepared are ones that the deceased enjoyed in their lifetime. "On Día de los Muertos, the dead are also a part of the community, awakened from their eternal sleep to share celebrations with their loved ones" (National Geographic, 2020, n.p.). This holiday is not a somber remembrance. Rather, it serves to unite everyone in the important universal life experience of death. The dead are not forgotten. The survivors are not alone in their grief and remembrance. Everyone experiences loss; this is part of the life experience. The whole community remembers the universality of death in a joyful two-day celebration.

Remembering is important.

The revered Buddhist Monk Thich Nath Hanh describes a Vietnamese tradition: "In Vietnam we have a tradition of worshipping our ancestors. Every family has an altar in their home. Every day people offer a stick of incense to their ancestors to help connect to their heritage. It only takes a minute..." (Hanh, 2014, n.p.). This daily ritual connects the present with the past and even points to the future. If you would like to practice this ritual, you do not have to have an altar, per se, but maybe a shelf in your home with pictures or memorabilia of your deceased loved ones. Simply bow to your loved ones and ancestors or ring a bell in reverence and appreciation. You can ask for a blessing for your day or a special event or a journey. When day is done, or when you return from your journey, again you can bow in reverence to your loved ones.

Those who are dear to us do not leave us. Their lives are a part of us. By honoring their memory and subtle presence in the form of pictures and memorabilia, dreams, and shared stories, we feel protected and guided. Cultures that honor the dead help the community to honor this bond. These remembrance rituals help us not to feel so alone in our grief and remind us that those who have died have a place in our hearts and in our life's journey.

Many Vietnamese people take pictures at funerals and wakes to remember the deceased. Li Nguyen, blog author of "Stories, Thoughts, Reviews and Whatnots," said,

> To Americans, talking about death is taboo, but to my family, it's connecting a duality. Death is just as much a part of life as is the reverse, a delicate interwoven tapestry. There is a balance as fine as a silk thread that has long been revered by us. When we take pictures of funerals or wakes, it's not to be macabre but more like a quiet reverence. The pictures show (that) the deceased was just as important in death as when they were alive. When we are older and our memories begin to fail, we are comforted knowing that we have our pictures to show us the full panoramic view of our loved one's life (2009, n.p.).

Community participation is required.

Hosea L. Perry, in his studies of African American funeral customs, found that African Americans typically encourage everyone to attend the funeral. Whether you are an immediate member of the family, a distant relative or friend, a colleague, a neighbor, or simply an acquaintance, your presence is required. It is a social obligation (Perry, 1993). In the Mexican American community, attendance by all is encouraged, too. How many times have we heard someone say, "I didn't know the person well, so I did not go to the funeral?"

When my brother died, two of my close friends attended the funeral. They did not know my family or my brother, but they did know me. Their attendance meant so much to me. At a time when I felt bereft, there they were. They connected me to the love beyond my family and beyond the grief we were feeling. I will always remember their kindness and their presence.

Judaism has the custom of Sitting Shiva. Shiva means seven. For seven days following a death, people visit, bring food, reminisce, and comfort the survivors.

The mourner's participation is required.

Some cultures have rituals and behaviors that are meant to help the deceased on his way to the afterlife or next life. Survivors are not lonely, powerless witnesses. They have a role to play. The secondary benefits of these behaviors are that they help the survivor and they help the community. The survivor may feel distraught, in shock, and alone, yet there is something that she can do to meaningfully participate in the loss. The mourner has a place in the death, and a place in the communal grieving process (Gloss & Klass, 1997). In New Orleans, the Jazz Funeral includes a walking funeral procession to mourn and celebrate the deceased person's life with music—at first solemn, but then joyful and lively.

In our modern culture, you may not be able to duplicate elaborate and meaningful grief rituals. However, you can create rituals that involve others in your loss, e.g., a meal celebrating your loved one's birthday; having informal remembrance events after the funeral such as enjoying an activity together that was special to the deceased; displaying photos of your loved one; going to the cemetery with family and friends; creating a memorial in honor of your loved one (roadside memorials commemorating a loved one who died in a car crash are now familiar to us); planning religious memorial events in addition to the funeral, creating a photo album or memory journal, and reminiscing with others.

How our culture is changing

Now that we have explored why grief can be lonely in Western culture and what we can learn from other cultures, let's look at the positive side of Western culture.

Our modern culture is in a state of change, exploration, and the study of new ideas. In 1969, Elisabeth Kübler-Ross's book *On Death and Dying* opened the eyes of the public to the subjects of death and dying. Then a year before her death in 2004, she and David Kessler explored the grief process in *On Grief and Grieving*.

In 1961, Granger Westberg, a chaplain and minister at the University of Chicago Divinity School and Medical School, was asked to give a sermon on grief at the Rockefeller Chapel, where many notable people had given sermons and lectures. His sermon was broadcast on the radio, and afterwards, a thousand positive letters came in. This was a record; usually the response from the public was about ten letters. Westberg thought that his preaching was working. So, the next time he was invited to preach, he gave a sermon on a different topic. This time, only a few letters came in. He then realized the importance of the topic of grief and how people were hungry for knowledge, for help, and for hope. He published his well-received sermon in a book titled *Good Grief* (2011) that is still in print today.

Our culture is youth-oriented. There is a good side to this: the desire to learn, to try new things, to meet new people, to live in the moment, to grow and change. No matter our age, we all have the capacity to reach out and connect with different people and to create bonds with people beyond our comfort zone.

We have roots, but we want rootedness.

We have cultural roots, but we may lack cultural rootedness, the rootedness that assures us that we belong, that we will make it, and that our actions are important and contribute to collective love and healing. We may feel lonely in a fast-moving culture. The feeling of loneliness diminishes our power. Hence, we reach out to one another, sometimes to complete strangers—people our ancestors would not have known or communicated with—to establish roots of love in the modern world. Like our ancestors, but without the encouragement of a supportive culture, we ask: Who am I? Why am I here? What is love? Will I survive? Will I be happy? What is life's meaning? Reaching out to others gives us new roots and enhances our sense of belonging.

In the 1960's, support groups were rare. "I don't need therapy." "People will think I am crazy if I join a group." These were typical responses to the suggestion to join a support group. Support groups are therapeutic, but they are not therapy. As communities became more fragmented, support groups became more accepted. You can now find support groups for just about everything, including grief. Members can meet in person and chat online, too. Support groups bring together total strangers who have an immediate bond based on a pivotal event in their lives. Frequently friendships evolve, and a new community is created.

We are creating a community of caring knowledge.

Elisabeth Kübler-Ross worked to bring death into our public consciousness. As a result, the medical profession has become less secretive and now discloses more information to the patient and family. Kübler-Ross was instrumental in starting the hospice movement in this country, where those who are dying receive comfort care and the cessation of active treatment for diseases in which the prognosis is six months or less. Her work began to change how we view illness, death, and grief.

Since then, medical diagnoses such as cancer, Alzheimer's disease, alcoholism, AIDS—diseases that in the not so distant past were shrouded in silence, misinformation, and frequently, shame—have become visible to the public and are openly discussed. Groups now champion medical causes. Notably, the Susan Komen Race for the Cure champions research for a cure for breast cancer, and champions those who are living with cancer.

In his book, *Being Mortal*, surgeon and author Atul Gawande, MD, says, "Medical professionals concentrate on repair of health, not sustenance of the soul" (2014, p. 128). He warns that encouraging and even pressuring the patient to do all that is medically possible may compromise the patient's quality of life and the lives of family members, too. Treating an illness includes enhancing the patient's psychological and social well-being and taking into consideration his wishes and goals. The doctor and the patient can work together in a collaborative way.

While Kübler-Ross was studying death, Phyllis Silverman (2004) was studying spousal grief. She asked widows if six weeks—the common belief at that time—was how long it took them to overcome their grief. The emphatic answer was No! Two years, if you were lucky, was the overwhelming response. What helped the widowed person the most? Counselors? Therapists? No. Other widowed people, because they understood the experience. She helped to start a widow-to-widow group where trained widowed volunteers helped newly widowed people, in one-on-

one settings, support groups, social gatherings, and educational events. Her pioneering work brought individual grief into the open. Grief is not something to be glossed over and forgotten, a short, dreaded experience. It is part of the human experience, and we, as friends, neighbors, and colleagues, can help one another when it happens.

These three phenomena—removing the secrecy and shame about death, honoring grief as an important universal experience, and the ongoing change from authoritarian to collaborative medicine—continue to evolve and help bring us together.

Presently, there is a growing body of information on grief. Let's call it a community of knowledge. For years, authors wrote about the many different stages of grief. Although some researchers still see merit in the stage model of grief, many are moving away from it. Bereavement therapy was honored as the best way to help people. Today, studies reveal that grief therapy does not always help the normal griever and may be harmful. Consequently, many therapists are revising their methods to primarily help only those whose grief is intractable and never-ending. Grief is a natural part of life. The number of years for one's grief to finish? Two years? Not necessarily. It can be a short period of time or a long one. Since the 1960's, many people have added to the field of grief and to our understanding. Many have devoted their lives to the study of grief. Some tell their own grief stories to help themselves and others.

This complex discussion may seem overwhelming. Juan Enriquez, businessperson and author, says, "…when you think of how much data is coming into our brains, we are trying to take in as much data in a day as people used to take in in a lifetime" (2015, n. p.). Rather than be overwhelmed, listen to your inner heart. Deep inside, you know what will help you, what resonates with your inner spirit. This will be different for each person and true for each person.

Chapter Summary

In the 19th and early 20th centuries, people lived in communities where everyone was known. Your loss was known by all. Death was common among all ages, particularly among young people. The doctor might have been able to diagnose your problem but could seldom provide a cure.

In the early 20th century, dramatic advances in medicine helped people to survive to adulthood and old age. Death became much less common among younger people. At the same time, the migration to urban areas improved job opportunities and led to the creation of many sub-communities. No longer would everyone know when you had experienced a loss. With lower early mortality rates, many people did not necessarily know how to be of help to someone who was grieving.

We can learn from other cultures. Death is not a failure or endpoint but a natural part of life. Many cultures include the bereaved in funeral, burial, and memorial rituals. Their participation helps the soul on its journey and unites the community around the loss. Survivors are not just witnesses. Instead, they have a significant role to play in the funeral and other remembrance services. Remembering the deceased on a regular basis is a way to link us with those who have died, e.g., annual celebrations of the deceased, and ancestor worship.

Our culture is changing, too. In the 1960's we began to accept that illness, death, and grief are a natural part of life. Doctors began to share more information and options with patients and families. People began to see that grief is important and can last longer than six weeks. This slow and important journey of change continues to this day.

Many professionals and grieving people alike are creating a different kind of community – a community of caring knowledge.

Chapter 3

The Experience of Grief and What It Might be Like for You

"I was just as crazy as you can be and still be at large. I didn't have any really normal minutes during those two years. It wasn't just grief. It was total confusion. I was nutty...."
—*Helen Hayes*[3]

Your individual grief experiences will differ from others' experiences and differ from your own past grief experiences. When you lose someone, your experience of the loss may surprise you. You might envision how you might feel, or what you might think, but you will not know how you are with the loss until it happens.

The experience of grief includes general characteristics commonly experienced by everyone and personal characteristics that are particular to your own situation. Your personal characteristics will affect how you experience the more general characteristics. All these characteristics are interwoven.

Five general characteristics

There are five general characteristics of grief that by and large we all experience. They are the search for meaning, the dual process of grief, oscillation in grief, reminders, and middle knowledge. Not everyone experiences these in the same way.

---

3   As cited in McNees (1996, p. 167).

Search for meaning.

As human beings, we search for meaning, and we create meaning. We are meaning-making animals. The way we make meaning of death is the same way we make meaning of life—through stories.

- We listen to stories.
- We tell stories.
- We create meaning through stories.
- We come to understand through stories.
- We feel a part of life by sharing stories.

Guy A. M. Widdershoven, Professor of Philosophy and Ethics of Medicine and head of the Department of Medical Humanities at Amsterdam University Medical Center, Amsterdam, the Netherlands, says "...life is both more and less a story. It is more in that it is a basis for a variety of stories and it is less in that it is unfinished and unclear as long as there are no stories told about it. The intertwining of experience and story lies at the core of individual life and psychological understanding" (1993, p. 19).

How many times have we been at a funeral of a loved one where someone tells us a story about him, a story that until that moment we did not know? We are uplifted by this knowledge, this story.

When a loved one or even an enemy dies, there is a need to make sense of the death. Why did it happen? How did it happen? Could it have been prevented or avoided? What was the chronology of events leading up to the death? Was his death peaceful? What were his last words? Your efforts to find the answers to these questions help you to pull together the story of what happened so that you can tell it.

And then there is your story. What did your loved one's life mean to you? What is the meaning of your own life now that your loved one is gone? What is the meaning of your loved one's life? What is the meaning of your loved one's death? What is the meaning of life now?

The search for medical answers, spiritual answers, and personal answers is part of the quest for meaning. Telling the story of your loved one and telling your own story help you to discover meaning in the loss. Over time, the stories may change and evolve. This is not to say that the old stories were false. Rather, over time, as you change, you may discover facets of the stories that may not have been known or may not have seemed important or relevant before. As you change and grow, your understanding, wisdom, and compassion may cast a new light on the past.

The dual process of grief

Margaret Stroebe and Henk Schut, psychologists, developed the dual process theory of grief. They recognize that you are grieving, and you are also learning new skills as you move on in your life. A dual process is happening (Stroebe, Schut, & Stroebe, 2005).

In grief, you may feel very alone, maybe even crazy, ashamed, angry, fearful, guilty, and hopeless. Your sense of who you are is turned upside-down. Yesterday you were a spouse. Today you are a widower. Yesterday you were someone's child. Now you are orphan. You may feel that no one understands or cares. You may make irrational decisions and be upsetting to yourself and others. You may accept that your loved one is dead and then at another time be sure that you saw her. This is intense grief.

Yet, other things happen: you continue your practical daily life by going to work and carrying out your household duties. You may be grateful for those who "get it" and respect your experience. You may make new friends, discover new skills, experience episodes of joy, and become stronger.

Grief is a process in which you recognize and adjust to your loss, incorporate it into your life, and move on in your life. The loss entails more than the absence of a person you love. It can also include a change in your identity and roles, a loss of safety, a loss of meaning, and a changed view of your world. You grieve the loss of your loved one, and you grieve the loss of your own place in the world. You have to come to terms with these two losses:

One is the interior loss: What does the loss of this person mean to me? How will I make it without him?

The other is the outer loss: How will I now make my way in the world?

A dual process is happening: adjusting to your loss and making it in the world in a new way. These two things, by and large, do not happen simultaneously. You go back and forth between the pain and stress of grief, and the challenge of making a new life. You oscillate between the two.

Oscillation in grief

Hopefully, you will not be grieving 24/7. Hopefully, you won't be doing anything 24/7. We all take breaks from what we are doing to give ourselves respite: to replenish, rejuvenate, and restore a sense of equilibrium. This is called oscillation. It is no different in grief. There will be times when you need to attend to other activities. You oscillate, or go back and forth, between experiencing the pain of grief and going about other activities, including experiencing other non-grief feelings and thoughts.

Oscillation can happen naturally. It can start simply as a matter of attention. Unwillingly, one's attention focuses on a new life almost immediately. After her spouse's death, the widowed spouse unwillingly eats alone, sleeps alone, and wakes up alone. The new life starts, but it is not a creation. It is simply attempting to attend to the daily matters of life.

Circumstances may demand oscillation. In your day-to-day life, you may need to learn new skills that were performed by the deceased and thus focus on your learning. If your job requires human interaction and/or a lot of concentration, you may find it necessary to simply perform your duties as best as you can.

Oscillation can be willed. You may need a breather from grief and create welcome opportunities to think about other things or engage in other activities that bring pleasure. A 92-year-old widower was interviewed on the PBS NewsHour. After his wife of over 60 years died, he felt that "something vital has gone out of my life." He was asked if he missed his wife every day. "Pretty nearly every day. Every once in a while, I take a day off" (Goldbloom, 2017, n.p.).

If you are with people with whom you are uncomfortable or who do not understand, or who wish you were over it, you may opt to put your grief on hold until those encounters end. On the other hand, you can avoid those people for a time.

Sometimes, desired oscillation will not happen. You may decide that at work you cannot cry, you can only work. Suddenly, you burst into tears. Or you attend an event to take a break from your grief and memories come back, and grief washes over you.

At other times, you may experience joy and contentment when you are engaged in some activities. Relish these times as they will give you strength.

Human beings are wired for grief (Bonanno, 2009). It is natural for us to grieve our losses and to continue with our lives.

We are also wired for love. It is natural for us to love and to continue with our lives.

We are wired for movement. It is natural for us to move and to rest.

Oscillation occurs naturally in our human behaviors. With oscillation, we achieve equilibrium (Bonanno, 2009). With oscillation, we grow. It may seem that we are compartmentalizing by doing one thing and then the other, but each will have an effect on the other. There is give-and-take. Your grief will color the rest of your life, and your life will color your grief. It reminds me of "Ecclesiastes" in the *Old Testament*. There is a season for everything under heaven.

Reminders

A reminder (Rosenblatt, 1983) is anything that reminds you about your loss and triggers a grief experience: holidays, birthdays, an aroma, a room in a house, a place, an event, a favorite restaurant, or an article of clothing. You can sometimes see reminders coming and prepare for them, e.g., not being alone (or being alone) on special anniversary dates. What are your reminders?

With time, reminders may not trigger intense grief reactions. Instead, they will rejuvenate the bond between you and your loved one and may give you hope and a sense of peace.

Middle knowledge

Avery Weisman, a psychiatrist, who studied human dying, identified middle knowledge as the "fluctuation between denial and acceptance" (1972, p. 65). (Parkes and Prigerson call this "double knowledge" [2010, p. 75].) Middle knowledge can occur during the dying process. You may know that your loved one is dying, but then, there might be another treatment to try, or a far-in-the-future event to look forward to.

In mourning, middle knowledge may manifest in this way: you grieve the loss of your loved one, and then forget that she died and call her on the phone or set a place for her at the table. You straddle the fence of reality. On the one hand, you grieve your loss. And on the other hand, it didn't happen. This is natural, and a way we slowly assimilate difficult knowledge.

In the beginning, there may be only shock and disbelief. The yes-no of middle knowledge evolves after the shock has worn off.

One widow, whose husband had been dead for a year, described her experience this way: "I was proud of myself for making it through the year. When the year ended and I had gone through the last of the first times for everything, I inwardly said to him, 'Okay, I made it through the year. You can come back now.'"

Author Joan Didion gave away her deceased husband's clothes but could not give away his shoes: "...he would need them if he were to return. The recognition of this thought has by no means eradicated the thought. I still have not tried to determine (say, by giving away the shoes) if the thought has lost its power" (2005, p. 25).

Six personal characteristics that make your grief unique

Your personal characteristics affect how you will experience grief. By their very nature, each of these characteristics is unique to you and your situation.

Let's look at six personal characteristics:

1. An expected death or a sudden death
2. Attachment: how attached you were to the deceased
3. Identity and roles: how much they changed because of your loss
4. Changes in your view of the world (your view of the world, your "take" on it is called your assumptive world)
5. Judgment: your susceptibility to the judgments of yourself and others
6. Your psychological strengths and weaknesses

An expected death or a sudden death

When a death is expected, you have time to prepare, share final sentiments, and to grieve. When a death is sudden, there is no time to prepare and no opportunity to say goodbye. A sudden death may also be a traumatic death, such as a homicide or a suicide—leaving the survivors themselves in a traumatized state.

Even in an expected death, there can be suddenness in its finality. No matter how much you as a loved one are prepared, there is a shock in that last leap, that last moment. Further, aspects of the dying process or the death itself for which you were not prepared may be traumatic.

Attachment: how attached you were to the deceased

Attachment is defined as "a personal connection or feeling of kinship" (yourdictionary.com, n.p.). Grieving people allude to the importance of attachment. They may say that after the death of a loved one, "I feel like I am missing a limb," or "There is a hole in my heart."

If you did everything together, your grieving experience may be different from those who had a mixture of shared and separate interests. You may not even realize how attached you are until death separates you.

John Bowlby, psychologist and psychiatrist, researched attachment, particularly in human infants and their mothers. When separated from Mom, the baby becomes distressed and will cry and search for her. Over time, the baby's distress between Mom's leaving and returning will lessen as the baby's trust and sense of safety increases.

Bowlby saw that attachment behaviors have their roots in infancy and are experienced throughout the lifespan. The baby behaviors when an attachment figure is gone occur in adults, too—crying, searching, and exhibiting distress. "In sickness and calamity, adults often become demanding of others; in conditions of sudden danger or disaster a person will almost certainly seek proximity to another known and trusted person" (1982, p. 208). In death, that very person who you may have turned to in times of distress is no longer there.

The attachment may be to a person with whom you had a trusting and loving relationship. Or it could be to a person with whom you had a turbulent and mistrustful relationship. Or it could be a combination of the two. The attachment can be generational. Your last relative or your last friend may die, accentuating your aloneness and the end of the collective memory of your generation.

Identity and roles: how much they changed because of your loss

First, foremost, and most important, your identity is as a human being. There is no one else exactly like you. Whether you are a baby or an older person, or at any of the different ages in between, you are unique; you are special.

You live in the world with other human beings, and you have many identities in your daily life. Certain identities are assigned to you: e.g., sibling, niece, nephew, child, grandchild, grandparent, ethnicity, nationality, gender, age, the religion you were born into, and your family of origin. Others are identities you create: spouse, lover, parent, friend or colleague, neighbor, retiree, working person, your acquired knowledge and skills, and your philosophy and/or chosen religion.

When a loved one dies, you miss the person and you miss your identity as a spouse, child, parent, or friend. You may miss the roles you played and all the things you did to maintain and enhance the relationship. For example, a parent may cook meals, work to support the family, shop, pay bills and maintain finances, be a chauffeur, oversee and support school progress, read stories, teach values and skills, mediate disputes, celebrate family events, give and receive love, and more. If your child dies, many of these roles will either stop or drastically change.

The following exercise demonstrates how important identities and roles are for each of us. When these change, the effect can be jarring and even devastating. As you read the following "I" sentences, experience each assertion of identity. Then, when you read the next sentence, imagine the distress that can so easily challenge who we think we are.

- I am a good wife. My spouse dies.
- I am a good husband. My spouse has an affair.
- I am a competent worker. I didn't get the job.
- I am a hard worker. I was fired.
- I am healthy. I was diagnosed with cancer.
- I am graceful and energetic. I fell and broke my hip.
- I am safe and carefree. I am the victim of human violence.
- I am a soul mate to my lover. She now is living with Alzheimer's disease.
- I am a good parent and protect my children. My child dies.
- I am a competent driver. I caused an auto accident.

Changes in your view of the world

Your worldview is called your assumptive world: what you assume you will see when you wake up in the morning, and who will be there. If you can attach the word *my* or *our* to someone or something, that is your assumptive world.

When your loved one dies, your assumptive world changes. In sudden death, you do not see the change coming. Your assumptive world can change completely in one second. The more your assumptive world changes because of your loss, the more you have to adjust to the change and rebuild your life.

In the United States, the assassinations of prominent and/or vulnerable persons and the terrorist attacks of 9/11 have occurred within our current historic memory. Our assumptive world as a society has changed.

We even connect strongly with past historic tragedies that affected generations long ago, before we were born. I attended a play about Mary Todd Lincoln, staged in the theatre where Lincoln was assassinated. It was about her experience as a newly widowed person. As the final curtain came down, many people were weeping. Our collective consciousness is still incorporating that tragic loss into our American assumptive world even though it occurred over 150 years ago, on April 15, 1865.

Your assumptive world can even include strangers. Few of us knew those who died on 9/11, yet that terrorist attack affected all Americans. We felt a connection to the victims and their surviving families.

The connection may not even be with a human. You can have a connection to the natural world. For example, when I learn of the decimation of elephants for ivory, I am devastated. I personally don't know a single elephant, but they are part of my assumptive world.

Frequently, grieving people cut back on their TV viewing or Internet news consumption. The news always has losses in it and may further affect and change your assumptive world.

Another characteristic of our assumptive world that most of us share is that death is optional. "For most people, death is a fateful and regrettable necessity. Yet, they harbor a primitive belief that appeal is possible, that suitable negotiation is available, and that, granted the forbearance of adversaries, death might not, after all, be compulsory" (Weisman, 1972, p. 6). When death happens to significant others in your life, suddenly the door to the possibility of your own death is opened, maybe just a crack, and to the possibility of the deaths of others who are dear to you.

Judgment: your susceptibility to the judgments of others and yourself

How do others judge your grief? How do you judge your grief?

In the *Talmud*, it is said, "Hold no man responsible for his utterances in times of grief" (Palano, 2009, p. 291). Let's paraphrase that: One must give up judgment about everything a human being experiences in grief unless it is violent or destructive.

It is easy for most of us to accept that there are different levels of love. You may be closer to one family member and less close to another. You may have different degrees of love and different expressions of love for your friends. Somehow with grief, we mistakenly think that we should experience it a certain way, and if we don't, we wonder if we are grieving correctly.

Your regular ways of thinking, feeling, and acting may no longer work for you. You may find yourself looking to others for validation of what you are experiencing. Rather than simply appreciating what you are going through, others may instead judge your experience and offer advice on what you should or should not be experiencing. This is hard to take.

Kathleen R. Gilbert (1996), educator and researcher in family studies, says,

> One of the assumptions held by family members may be that because they have lost the same individual their grief should be the same. Alternatively, some may also assume a shared view that their experience of the loss is more significant than that of other family members, or that they have suffered more because of the relationship they shared with the deceased. They may also believe that the loss was less significant for themselves than for others and feel uncomfortable with the expectation that they should 'put on a show of feelings' to accommodate other family members. Finally, because they need to socially confirm the reality of the loss and its impact on their assumptive world, family members may presuppose greater similarity in beliefs within the family than may actually exist.... Some may see the loss as devastating; others may see it as distressing; yet others may find it a relief. An additional

complication is that, over time, individual members may experience changes in their own interpretation of the loss (p. 276).

Grief is not a contest as to who loves the best, or who grieves the best, although the opinions and words of others can make you feel that way. One of the challenges of grief is that you may feel scrutinized by others: you are not grieving correctly, you are crying too much or not at all, or you are grieving for too long or for too short a period.

In grief, it is hard to know who you are so if you want to be yourself that may be impossible. Instead, have an intention to accept yourself. Give yourself permission to experience your loss in your own way. Give everyone else that permission, too. In families, communities, or friend groups, you all may share the loss, but you will not share the same grief (Gilbert, 1996). Your grief and its expressions are yours alone.

Your psychological strengths and weaknesses

Your own personal psychological history affects how you engage with the world. Your engagement is not static. You change, grow, and learn from your life experiences.

You have strengths and weaknesses, and they manifest in challenging times, oftentimes in surprising ways. You might think that you have zero self-confidence and that this is a weakness. However, in grief this "weakness" could inspire you to ask for help from others and talk with others about how you are doing. On the other hand, you may think that knowing the answers to life is your strength. In grief, maybe suddenly there are no answers, and now "knowing the answers" is no longer a "strength." It may not even be possible.

The psychological strengths and weaknesses you possess may be different depending on your age. The needs of a young child who loses a parent differ from those of a middle-aged adult who loses a parent. Hopefully, the bereft adult will be able to function independently in the world without his parent. Of course, this same level of independence would not be expected of a grieving child.

How did you manage other losses and life challenges? Are there losses that have stayed with you for a long time and have had a long-term effect on you? Do you have a support system that you can depend on, or are there few people to talk to about your experience? The answers to these questions are part of your psychological and social makeup.

Julie Potter, MSW, LCSW

Chapter Summary

There are five general characteristics that are part of the human experience of grief:

1. *Search for meaning.* The search for and appreciation of the meaning of life is a universal human quality. We discover meaning through stories—the stories we tell and the stories we listen to.

2. *The dual process of grief.* A necessary dual process is happening: the process of grieving your loss and the process of creating a new life. Each of these requires a different kind of energy. One is interior and personal; the other is exterior and an engagement with the world.

3. *Oscillation.* You go back and forth between grieving your loss, then attending to other activities and life responsibilities.

4. *Reminders.* These are places, events, people and things that bring on or "trigger" a grief experience. They can be traditional such as birthdays or anniversary events or something as simple as a song on the radio.

5. *Middle knowledge.* One knows and does not know that the loss has occurred. You may have times when you completely forget that your loved one died. Middle knowledge helps you to take in difficult knowledge slowly.

There are six personal characteristics that make your experience of grief unique:

1. *An expected or sudden death.* If the death was expected, you had time to prepare. If it was sudden, there was no preparation, and possibly the loss has elements of trauma for you. Even in an expected death, there may be elements of suddenness.

2. *Attachment* - how attached you were to the deceased. An adult whose parent dies will have a different kind of attachment than a child whose parent dies. How much you grieve will depend on how attached you were to that person.

3. *Identity and roles,* and how much they changed because of your loss. Each loss has some amount of identity and role change.

These can be acutely felt. The death of a child and the death of a spouse are losses that cause extensive and deep changes.

4. *Changes in your view of the world.* Your view and experience of the world is called your assumptive world. When your loved one dies, this changes –sometimes dramatically.
5. *Judgment* - your susceptibility to the judgments of yourself and others. In their wish to help, people may be critical of how you are, or are not, grieving. You, too, may judge your grief, and wish that you could be different.
6. *Your psychological strengths and weaknesses.* The strengths and weaknesses that you possess will affect your grieving process. These strengths and weaknesses can change over your lifespan.

Your own personal characteristics will affect how you experience the more general characteristics of grief. Learning about these characteristics may help you to understand and appreciate your grief experience.

Julie Potter, MSW, LCSW

Part 2
THE TASKS OF GRIEF:
What you do to make it through

Part 2 includes a discussion of the four tasks of grief, how you can complete them, and how you may revisit them throughout your life.

Note that I have divided task 2 into four chapters for ease of reading. In this way, you can focus on the experiences of pain one at a time.

The tasks give you an idea of the big picture of your grief. As you make progress on one task, you may find that you are making progress on the others as well. Your picture of your own grief then changes.

The tasks are interwoven. They do not stand alone. For example, task 2 is to experience the pain of grief. Yet pain is woven into the other tasks too. Each task can be painful!

Julie Potter, MSW, LCSW

Chapter 4

Task 1: To Accept the Reality of the Loss

"It feels like being mildly drunk, or concussed. There is a sort of invisible blanket between the world and me. I find it hard to take in what anyone says."
—*C.S. Lewis*

How many times have we said, or heard, "I can't believe she died?" The knowledge of your loved one's death has to become real to you. It may take some time for the knowledge to sink in.

There is no way to predict how you will respond initially to a loss. You may feel devastated and in shock. The loss may seem unreal, surreal, like you are in a daze. Or you may not feel anything that could be identified as grief. You may have compassion for the person who died, and that may be the extent of it. Whether you are alone or surrounded by people who are of help to you, the implications of the loss may not sink in right away.

In the event of sudden, violent, or traumatic death, other conditions may complicate accepting the loss: the involvement of the coroner, medical personnel, law enforcement, the judicial system, and/or the media.

Before and after the services, you may be busy with death-related details such as the obituary, death notices, and notification of family and friends' details that bring home the reality of the loss. Middle knowledge may be frequent at this time: one minute you know it happened, the next minute, you don't. Slowly, the knowing times become longer and the not-knowing times shorter.

Julie Potter, MSW, LCSW

How to accept the reality of the loss

There are a number of different things you can do to accept the reality of the loss.

Attend funeral and memorial services.

Viewings, wakes, funerals, memorial services, and graveside services are powerful interactive events that help you to accept the reality of the loss. These events are our culture's way of publicly acknowledging that the death has occurred, of providing comfort and support to the survivors, of bringing solemnity and sacredness to the event, and of honoring the deceased.

It is good to attend funerals, no matter what your relationship was with the deceased. All the people you know are a part of your life. I have been surprised by how moved I have felt at funerals where I have limited knowledge of the deceased and his community or where I may only know the survivors. Your presence at a funeral is a form of respect for the passing of a human life, for the survivors, and for the integrity of your community. Your presence contributes to the completeness of your community and is a comfort to mourners. In many cases, your attendance may be enough for you to accept the reality of the loss.

The entire process of the funeral, from the viewing or wake, to the service, internment, and then perhaps a meal or gathering afterwards, symbolizes what has happened and what will happen. The death has happened. We honor the person who has died, and we comfort one another. We return to our lives changed. Theresa Rando, a clinical psychologist specializing in grief education and grief therapy, describes the importance of the funeral: "As a rite of passage, the funeral assists you in recognizing the passing of your loved one, supporting you as you start your life without the deceased, and reintegrating you back into the social group as a person whose loved one is no longer alive. A funeral can mark the beginning of your new social identity" (1991, p. 266).

Many people find that the viewing of the body is helpful. For others, seeing the closed casket or urn is helpful. A photo or a collage of photos and testimonials inspire conversation and memories about the deceased.

People may decide against a funeral service—if the death was violent, such as homicide or suicide, if there was an estranged or difficult relationship with the deceased, or if perhaps there were financial difficulties that might preclude funeral arrangements. If there are services, you may choose not to attend if your relationship with the deceased was a secret, for example, a lover.

If you choose not to have a funeral service, there are other ways to acknowledge the death. Do something to memorialize your loved one. Perhaps have a gathering of friends and family where each person will offer support and/or share a story about the deceased. Plant a tree as a memorial. Display a photo of your loved one. Make up a simple ritual of remembrance. At any gathering of family or friends, you can make an opportunity for remembrance. Bring up the person's name, or tell a story about him, a "Remember When?" story. Write a letter of gratitude and appreciation to your deceased loved one.

Talk about your loss.

Repeat the story of what happened. Remembering and recounting the accurate chronology of events, whether the death is anticipated or sudden, can help you accept the reality of the loss.

- What happened?
- When did it happen?
- What happened first?
- What happened next?
- Who was there?
- What were your last words to your loved one?
- What were his last words?
- Was there anything special about the day?
- Or the day before?

When a death is expected, the chronology of events unfolds slowly. There is the opportunity for each event to be acknowledged in sequence. For many, a serious or life-threatening illness does not necessarily mean that you as the survivor were ready for your loved one's death. There was still the hope that he would survive and get better. When your loved one then dies, the chronology of events is now seen in a different light. Each event and each word now take on a different significance—as the precursor to death rather than the path to health.

Talking with others may sometimes be difficult. Some conversations dilute or take you away from your own experience. Suddenly, it's their experience. They might say, "I know exactly how you feel." Or, "The same thing happened to me." They do not know exactly how you feel, and the same thing did not happen to them. There may be similarities, but your experience is unique and needs to be honored.

The following two stories illustrate the strength of a grieving person's desire to talk even despite the difficulty in getting someone to listen.

> Right after my husband died, all I wanted to do was to talk about my loss. A neighbor came to the door and brought me a cake. I was very grateful for her company, and I invited her in. She said, "No, I just wanted to drop off this cake for you."
>
> I encouraged her and said, "Come on in, and have a cup of tea. I would love to talk with you."
>
> "No, I just wanted to drop off this cake for you." She gave a couple reasons why she couldn't stay.
>
> I tried one more time, but to no avail. Graciously, I thanked her and then bid her farewell.
>
> I desperately wanted to talk with someone. Even though I was upset, I realized my neighbor was just trying to help, but she wasn't helpful. I threw the cake out.
>
> —Mary Kate Cranston

Another person relates:

> My cousin committed suicide. During conversations, I would tell friends that he had died. When they asked what had happened, I would tell them, 'He committed suicide.' Time and again, right before my eyes, they would be shocked and would fall apart. I would find myself comforting them when it was I who needed the comfort. Seldom did I find someone who would just be there with me in silence. I got to the point where I didn't tell people about his death. It was too hard on me.

Write about your loss.

In the fascinating book, *The Cost of Hope*, journalist Amanda Bennett (2012) recounts the seven years she and her husband were joined in a battle for his survival from cancer. They just knew he would get better. He had several remissions, during which they enjoyed life immensely. Each time his disease reached a serious phase, he survived—until he didn't.

Bennett retells a final harrowing visit to the emergency room when the death of her husband was imminent but not obvious to her or him. While his situation was being assessed, a "27-year-old intern" dissuaded her from the idea of full resuscitation should he die and proposed the idea of hospice to her. Her response: Wasn't there something else that could be done? One more treatment that would help? She finally accepted hospice care and for the next several days until his death was at his bedside.

Bennett later interviewed all the doctors who took care of her husband during his long illness, elaborated on the cost of each treatment, and got their thinking on how they arrived at the diagnoses and why they prescribed the various treatments. She even interviewed the 27-year-old intern who was by then a doctor, to review that last ER encounter. She carefully reviewed the tapestry of her husband's illness, their love together, and the chronology of events leading to his death.

Few of us would have the time or the energy for such a journey, but as an author and a journalist, it was just what she needed to do. Did she have any regrets? "No, sad as I was at our silent farewell, I would not trade away any of those years of fighting for life" (Bennett, 2012, p. 222).

Were she and her husband in denial? No. Bennett says, they were in hope.

Bennett shared her own personal journey through Task 1. You do not have to write a book unless you are so inclined, but you can keep a journal. There is something powerful about the written word that conversation cannot reach. As you try to tell people what you are thinking and feeling, you may get well-intentioned responses that stop the conversation: "Don't feel that way." "Don't think that way." "Time will heal." "Things will get better." "It could have been worse." "You can remarry." Yet when you are writing, the conversation does not stop nor is it interrupted. When you are writing about your loss, you are writing to yourself. There is no hidden motive, such as to impress yourself or to change yourself. There is no weighing of words so as not to offend yourself. There is no waiting for a reaction or a validation from yourself. You are simply expressing yourself. You can just say it as you see it. Writing in this way deepens your appreciation of yourself. It helps you to be authentic. It increases your self-confidence and gives you power.

Visit the cemetery.

The cemetery is a sacred place of remembrance. Seeing your loved one's name on a stone or a niche brings home that your loved one has died. Cemetery visitations can be a deeply painful reminder. They can also bring comfort and a sense of connection with the deceased.

Make the best use of reminders.

Reminders are anything that reminds you of your loved one: a thought that comes up, a special event, an article of clothing, someone who looks like your loved one.

Reminders help us to acknowledge the reality of the loss and to incorporate the loss into our individual lives and into the lives of our communities.

Especially in the beginning, any reminder can be painful, reminding you vividly of your loved one's absence. Eventually, a reminder can be a source of comfort. Sudden and traumatic deaths may bring reminders that are terrifying and haunting. They may be too present. Finding ways to slow down their insistent presence may be helpful to you. (See Chapter 11).

The losses that carry few or no reminders can be harder on you. Some people may elect to quickly dispose of all the artifacts or clothing of the deceased. If you are inclined this way, save one or two items for a while, because later, these reminders can bring comfort. Many recommend not making big decisions during the first year after a loss. Giving away or disposing of items quickly may bring regret later. So, save a few items.

In the event of miscarriage, a stillbirth, an abortion, death at birth, or giving up an infant for adoption, there may be no reminders. If you feel you are not getting enough support from families and friends, find a support group or a counselor who can be of help.

Task 1 is not only for the close survivors of the deceased but also for the entire community. A well-known memorial that serves this purpose is the Vietnam Memorial in Washington, DC. Families, friends, and the public remember the deaths of soldiers during this war. The Holocaust Museum in Washington, DC, reminds the public that mass genocide of Jewish people indeed happened in Germany in World War II. Visiting the Vietnam Memorial and the Holocaust Museum helps us to face the reality of these massive events and losses.

As a society, we need to collectively remember and honor those who have died. All who have died are a part of our societal community. As described in Edward Ball's essay, "Retracing Slavery's Trail of Tears" (2015), tragedies that are suppressed are not real to us, and we are diminished by this suppression. Outside of Natchez, Mississippi, at an intersection called Forks of the Road, hundreds of enslaved people were sold every month during the Slave Trail of Tears, from 1810 to 1860. Cotton farming in the South was on the rise, and tobacco farming in the North was in decline. Consequently, one million enslaved people were marched to the Deep South during that time. Forks of the Road was the second largest slave market during that period, second only to New Orleans. Until 1999, it was just another street corner, with no public remembrance of that time in history. Thanks to the unremitting work of Ser Boxley, who was born in Natchez, Forks of the Road is becoming better known. To fellow African Americans, he says, "The way you transcend the hurt and the pain, is to face the situation, experience it and cleanse yourself, to allow the humanity of our ancestors and their suffering to wash through you and settle into your spirit" (n.p.).

Find ways to acknowledge the unacknowledged loss.

An unacknowledged loss is one that is important to you yet is minimized and underestimated by others, such as the death of a friend or colleague or a divorce.

The loss may be known only to you. You may have experienced a loss and may not feel free to talk with anyone about it, for instance, in cases of abuse, rape, suicide, or homicide. Many cultures, ours included, tend to blame the victim or the survivor. It is harder to accept the reality of the loss when you feel that others may blame you or when you blame yourself. You may interpret the silence of others as blaming. Embarrassment or fear of saying something wrong may also be the cause of their silence. You may need to take the risk and be the one to open the door for conversation.

If you think that you are being blamed for your loss, if you are not getting any support or understanding for your loss, or if your loss is a secret that you cannot share with anyone, you might consider joining a support group or seeking professional help.

Someone who is missing or whose body is missing.

It is hard to accept the reality of the loss if there is any possibility, even remote, that your loved one is not dead. If your loved one is missing—missing in military action, gone missing, or presumed dead in a plane crash or a natural disaster in which the body may not be found—it is natural for you as the survivor to wait for years, maybe even the rest of your life, for the remote possibility that your loved one will return or be found. You may not even realize that you are doing this until someone walks into the room who looks like your loved one.

In the instance of a missing person, it is normal to come to a point where you accept the reality of the loss and also maintain hope that your loved one will be found. Many people live with this paradox. This is called an ambiguous loss, addressed further in Chapter 12.

Revisit Task 1.

As we continue with our lives, a new awareness may appear about those who have gone before us. As we change and grow, our ideas of those in our personal history can change and grow too. We may revisit Task 1.

My grandmother and I were cordial to each other, but I would not characterize us as close. When she died, I did not recognize her death as a loss in my life. Then years later, when in my 60's (she had died when I was in my 20's), our family was sharing stories about her, how her parents were divorced when she was young, how she managed for 30 years after her husband died, how she always had such class and gave the impression of not having a care in the world, and how her laughter filled her tiny frame of 4 feet 9 inches. At that moment, I revisited Task 1. I connected with the essence of who she was, and I more fully appreciated her life in a new way. It was only then that I started to miss her, to acknowledge her death in my life, and to appreciate the role she played in my life— just being herself, teaching me how to sew, graciously accepting my visits to her, and sharing time together. For a wedding present, she had given me an occasional table, and I always enjoyed it. Now I really enjoy it!

Task 1 can be revisited throughout one's life with some regularity. When a young child loses a parent, he may revisit Task 1 at special times in his life, such as graduations, sports events, his own marriage, and similar events. When parents lose a child, their relationship as a parent does not end. At different times and on different occasions, they may think, "I wonder what my daughter would be doing now as a 20-year-old." "What would my son look like now?"

I was driving down the street and saw an elderly woman with a cane, a cute hat, and white slacks, walking down the street. She looked like my mother. My mother had been dead 25 years. I knew this. Still, I drove my car around the block so I could pass the woman one more time, but by the time I came to the spot where I had seen her, she was no longer there. Then, my mother's death came rushing back to me, and I faced it all over again, this time from a different perspective. I had changed over the years. I had become more patient and more compassionate than when she was alive. I felt deep appreciation for who she was and gratitude that she had been my mother. The things that I had identified as her faults were now simply human characteristics that added to her life.

Task 1 is to accept the reality of the loss. Even in the beginning of your grief process, you may learn new things about your loved one. Someone at the funeral service may share a story that, until that moment, you did not know. You then appreciate your loved one in a new way. This may very well happen intermittently throughout your life. You will learn something new about the deceased, or about the times that he lived in, or the challenges he faced, and then revisit Task 1. As you come to a deeper understanding of the deceased, you now may be grieving for a somewhat different person, based on your new knowledge. In addition, you may grow in your own personal knowledge and wisdom. As you change over the years, your view of the deceased may also change.

Chapter Summary

Task 1 is to accept the reality of the loss. In order to grieve a loss, you first have to know that it happened, and then this knowledge has to become real to you. The element of disbelief can last for a short time or a long time. It can also be intermittent and return at pivotal times in your life, not always with the same intensity.

There are many ways to accept the reality of the loss. A powerful way is the funeral and/or memorial service. All cultures provide ceremonies and rituals to honor the deceased, to support family and friends, to share stories about the deceased, and to say, "This death has happened."

After the funeral, you may find that visiting the cemetery reinforces the reality of your loss and reinforces your connection with your loved one in a new way.

Talk about it. Think about it. Write about it. Getting accurate information about the death, reviewing the chronology of events leading to the death, listening to, and telling stories about your loved one, receiving condolences—these are all ways that help you to gain knowledge and to help make the knowledge real.

Pay attention to reminders, anything that reminds you of your loved one. They may give you a sense of your loved one's presence and absence. Sometimes, they can plunge you into grief and despair. They can also give you hope and comfort: although my loved one is gone from me, no one can take away my reminders, which are my unique connection to her memory.

In the instance of violent or sudden death or if your loved one is missing, the reminders may be even more painful. You may feel the need to consciously filter them for a time so that they do not overwhelm you.

Revisit Task 1. Throughout your life, you may experience events that rekindle your grief, and you may choose to revisit Task 1.

Chapter 5

Task 2: To Experience the Pain of Grief—Experiencing the Pain of Anger and Fear

> *"Let us not look back in anger, nor forward in fear, but around us in awareness."*
> —James Thurber

When you experience a loss, your reality is changed, and your stability is threatened. You may feel both angry and afraid. It is not a good idea to eliminate these emotions. They are normal human emotions. Nevertheless, you can manage them and work with them so that they do not control your life.

First, I will give an overview of both anger and fear. Then, I will discuss these emotions separately and ways to manage them. Although they seem like separate emotions, in many ways they are interconnected. Many feel that anger is the result of fear. A classic example of this is the distraught and worried parent whose teenager comes home late. The parent's first reaction may not be relief and joy but rather anger, "Where were you?!" For our purposes, I will by-and-large talk about these emotions separately.

Overview of anger and fear

Anger and fear are normal and powerful emotions. Anger can help you to right a wrong. Fear can help you to avoid danger. These uses of anger and fear are good. But we are talking about the anger and fear that can make you do something that you may later regret or keep you from doing something that you want to do. We are talking about the experiences of anger and fear that signal to you that you are out of control, the anger and fear that have power over you. You "lose" your temper. You are "paralyzed" with fear. You may lose sleep, shut down, overreact, be anxious, and surprise people and yourself with outbursts that are not "you."

Yet, you are in control. You do have the power to experience these emotions and to deal with them. With time, they may go away on their own. In the meantime, there are things you can do to understand them, work with them, and regain your power over them.

Does fear come first? Does anger come first? Do they come together? Whatever comes first, what you are going through is hard to face. One of the main tenets of Buddhism is *dukkha* (*suffering*). As human beings, we will all experience *dukkha*. Mark Epstein, a psychiatrist and Buddhist practitioner, tells us that *dukkha* is a word in the Pali language: *du* means *hard* or *difficult*; *kha* means *face*; together they mean "hard to face" (2013, p. 12). Anger and fear can be our first responses when something happens that is hard to face.

In grief, when the emotions of anger and fear arise, we can:

- express our anger and fight;
- express our fear as we flee from threatening situations or thoughts;
- shut down and do nothing;
- tend to or take care of ourselves and others (Taylor, 2002);
- reach out to others for support; and/or
- reach inward for support.

Some common examples where anger and fear can arise:

Fear: A family moves into the house next door: Will I like them? Will they be good neighbors? Will I have to confront them about their behavior? Shall I reach out and bring them a food offering?

Fear: I have started a new job: Will I succeed? Will I fail? Will I be accepted? How can I fit in?

Anger and fear: You and I are arguing. Does our argument signal the end of our relationship, or, on the other hand, a need for conversation and repair?

Anger and fear: I am late picking up my preschooler at the end of the school day, because I was stuck in traffic. My preschooler greets me with her rage and tears. I comfort her.

If anger and fear show up in our day-to-day life changes and experiences, it makes sense that they will be present in grief, too.

Experiencing the pain of anger

Anger is a strong feeling of being upset or annoyed because of something that is wrong or "bad."

Who are grieving people most likely to get angry with? Grieving people get angry with:

- themselves;
- the medical profession;
- the hospital;
- the funeral director;
- family members, friends and neighbors;
- someone who caused the death, such as in the case of a homicide;
- the deceased person – a suicide, or reckless behavior such as substance abuse, that hastened his death;
- anyone who doesn't understand or appreciate what you are experiencing; and/or
- people who haven't experienced a similar loss.

Anger may show up as jealousy. Many widowed people talk about how hard it is to see couples spending time together. Bereaved parents find it hard to see happy intact families.

You may be angry with yourself for not having done enough to prevent the death, or angry with God for the illness and death of your loved one.

A grieving person may feel abandoned, and angry with her loved one for dying. She may feel abandoned by her friends and family, who cared about her at the funeral, who sent a condolence card, but who then disappeared because they expected that her life was back to normal. After that, they are not there for her. She may feel dismissed when people behave as if nothing has happened.

Anger is a normal emotion during grief. Sometimes, the way you are approached can cause anger.

A woman relates:

> When my friend died, someone asked me, "Have you been crying about your friend's death?"
>
> I had to say "no." I felt diminished by her question and by my answer. I felt she was implying that I was doing something wrong by not crying and that I wasn't grieving properly.
>
> Then, I felt angry at her and her possessiveness of my experience. My grief experience is my own, and no one can take it away from me, no matter what their opinion or judgment is. My love for my friend is expressed through my grief, and I don't have to explain my love. I don't have to explain my grief.

An angry reaction may bring short-term relief and a sense of vindication. There may be satisfaction in anger and the sharing of angry feelings. The satisfaction gained will at first give a sense of justice and safety and may even feel enjoyable, but as time goes on anger may alienate the griever from others, the very others who may be of help (Parkes and Prigerson, 2010).

Rollo May (1969), a psychologist and author, says that the opposite of love is not hatred; the opposite of love is apathy. I would also say that love's opposite is indifference. Keep this in mind when you are angry. Anger makes you feel like you want to write the person off and never see him again, maybe even sever the relationship or take it down a few notches. However, your anger may be closer to love than it feels. If the person or situation were not important to you, it is less likely you would be angry; you might not even notice the behavior or the situation. Knowing that your anger is a relative of love may help you in managing and expressing anger appropriately.

An AARP driver safety course instructor used to tell his class, "There will be times when you are on the road and someone cuts you off or drives in a way that challenges your sensibilities. You can react angrily and be right. But your angry justified action can also cause you or others to be injured." He encouraged forbearance. Anger is like a big SUV. It is exciting, you feel good in it, and it can work well—but it can also be hugely destructive.

To complicate matters, as human beings we do not always get angry with the people we are actually angry with. We might lash out at someone else who has little or nothing to do with the situation at hand. Angry feelings may just seem to pop up in your awareness. Someone may offer condolences to you, and you may feel angry at this, not comforted. Over time, and as you integrate the loss into your life, and with some self-effort, your anger will decrease.

You cannot always control angry outbursts. Nevertheless, the time you take to think about and work through your anger is time well spent. Realizing that these strong feelings are a normal human response to change may help you to accept the intensity of what you are feeling and may help you to work through them.

Experiencing the pain of fear

Fear—being afraid or worried—can appear in your grief in various forms, such as

- fear of being alone;
- fear of traveling alone;
- fear of the future;
- fear that I will not be taken care of;
- fear that I will die the same way my loved one died;
- fear of doing things that I used to do easily;
- fear of the unknown;
- fear of death;
- fear that I will forget my loved one;
- fear of change;
- fear that nothing will change;
- fear that I will be sad forever; and
- fear that I won't make it.

Your fears, whether realistic or not, are real to you. How will I manage? What if I am hurt? Can I figure this out?

When you are undergoing a profound change in your life, your fears may be more intense, and for a time, you may experience more of them.

What makes your fears overwhelming? When you feel them all at once, you think everything you fear will happen all at once. Perhaps one or two fearful things could happen, but not all of them, and not all at once, and usually not at all.

If you are in a fearful cycle, you may escape one fear, breathe a sigh of relief, and then brace yourself for the next one. In this way, fear can keep you stuck. As the psychologist Marc Schoen writes, "…fear ramps up our aversion to loss. In other words, we are less likely to take chances when we feel fear, and we are more likely to see the potential for negative outcomes than positive ones. We look for safety rather than positive change" (2014, p. 198).

How to manage anger and fear

Anger and fear are closely related. You may experience them separately and together. When you are afraid, you may also be angry, and vice versa. The following ideas are applicable to managing both emotions except in the few places where I have noted them separately.

Think and choose alternative ways of acting and being.

Simply thinking about your anger and fear may not be enough to go beyond them. You may get into a repetitious cycle of ruminating, i.e., going over and over the same thing in your mind. There is a time to think and a time to choose alternatives. The woman telling the following story was angry, and she thought about it for a long time. The incident she relates affected her deeply, and for several years she struggled with her thoughts.

> My husband died suddenly. I left the room, and when I returned, I found him collapsed on the floor. He was rushed to the hospital emergency room in an ambulance. For two hours, I waited in the waiting room. Finally, I was told that he had died. I went home. At 3 a.m., I was awakened by a call from a police officer, asking my permission for an autopsy on my husband's body. I refused and was told to discuss this with the coroner in the morning. In the

morning, I called the morgue and was told that he was not there. I was terrified. I called the hospital and was told his body was not there, either. For several anguished hours, his body was lost. I lost my husband, and the hospital lost his body. Any semblance of control I had was completely gone. Finally, the hospital found his body. But I was angry with the hospital then, and for a period of five years, I couldn't even walk in its door. And it was a hospital that had been a mainstay in my life.

She was stuck in her thinking for five years and was angry about what had happened. Then she chose an alternative way of being, and a constructive, joyous way to live.

One day I was at a very low point. My life had no meaning. I am an accomplished pianist but had not touched the keys in a long time. Finally, at a local gathering sponsored by my temple, a "Good Deeds Day," I was asked to play. I did; it was beautiful. My rabbi came up to me afterward and said, "When you help others, you help yourself. I wish you would share your talent with others." So, with some trepidation, I went back to my community hospital and auditioned to play for others. Now, I go to the same hospital every week and play in the lobby for people who, like me, have faced or are facing life challenges. My anger is over. I still remember the experience that I had. It is a part of my life, but it no longer has a hold on me. I am at peace. I have come full circle. It is not that I forget the incident. I remember, but life has now opened up to me again.

—Cerlene Rose

Use your imagination

When you think about your anger and fear, you may slip into rumination and get stuck. When you ruminate, you go over and over a problem in your mind without coming to a solution.

You can ruminate about your anger and fear, in a worried and judgmental state. Or, you can imagine alternatives. Norman Fischer, poet and Zen Buddhist priest, says, "If we really want to go beyond the surface of things to the deeply hidden, actual experience of being alive...we need imagination as an ally. The senses, reason, even our moral and emotional faculties are not enough." He describes imagination as an antidote to fantasy (2005, n. p.). Instead of fantasy, I prefer to use the word rumination in the context of grief.

> Rumination removes you from reality. Imagination connects you to reality.

> Rumination separates you from others. Imagination can connect you with others.

> Rumination is static and repetitive, which means that your mind thinks the same fearful and angry thoughts, and then those thoughts get stuck as if in a groove and repeat themselves in a never-ending circle. Imagination is focused on a way out of the groove and out of the circle.

Rather than feeling separate from your angry and fearful thoughts—which gives them power—you enter the reality of your thoughts and feelings, and imagine another way to be, and that gives you power.

What follows is a valuable two-part exercise to identify your anger and fear and then to use your power of imagination.

Part 1. Using Table 5.1, write down as many fearful and angry thoughts as you can think of. What keeps you up in the middle of the night? What thoughts are situational and may dissipate after an event? (For example, you may have a fear of crowds and need to work up energy to go to that family reunion. Or you may be facing an unpleasant confrontation with someone). Sometimes, writing down what you are fearful and angry about is enough to help you.

Table 5.1 Fears I am experiencing. Anger I am experiencing.	
Fears I am experiencing	Anger I am experiencing
1.	1.
2.	2.
3.	3.
4.	4.
5.	5.
6.	6.

Part 2. Here is where the imagination comes in. Using Tables 5.2 and 5.3, rewrite a few fearful and angry thoughts under the columns titled "My fearful ruminations" (Table 5.2) and "My angry ruminations" (Table 5.3). In a second column, "My imagination," write an imaginative way to experience and deal with these fearful and angry thoughts. I have filled in a few fear and anger blanks just to get you started. Please add your own to this list.

Table 5.2
Fearful ruminations and the power of imagination

My fearful ruminations	My imagination
I will forget my loved one	I will celebrate my loved one's life through rituals that I will imagine – a displayed photo, talking about him to others, reminiscing about him with loved ones.
I will die alone. No one will be there for me.	I will live my life as fully as possible and will trust that all will be well at the end of my life.
I'm afraid of traveling alone	I will try a Smithsonian trip to get me started traveling alone but in the company of like-minded travelers.
I won't be able to make it on my own.	I don't have to make it on my own. There are resources that are available: friends, counseling, support groups.

Table 5.3
Angry ruminations and the power of imagination

My angry ruminations	My imagination
I'm angry with my friends who seem to dismiss my grief and seem to forget what has happened.	My friends are not evil, just insensitive. Or maybe afraid to talk to me. For now, I will seek out people who are sympathetic.
I am angry with myself. How did I miss the signs of approaching death?	I did the best I could with the information that I had.
I am angry with the medical profession. They should have done more/less.	I will talk with the medical team about the whole picture of my loved one's condition.
I am angry with the drunk driver who caused my child's death.	I will join a group, or donate to a group, that provides help so that others will not die the way my child died.

Stop thinking.

George Bonanno (2009) interviewed people who came to terms with their grief. Many of them reported that at times, they quite naturally stopped thinking about their grief or about the challenges they were facing. They oscillated between thinking and not thinking.

You can also choose not to think. You can choose to not think about your anger with the person who chronically says something inane. You can choose to not think about your fears when you feel helpless. (Parents do this a lot. Their adventurous teen is on a mountain-climbing trip, a date, or an errand in your car, and, yes, terrible things could happen. The parent sees the terror-filled thoughts piling up and simply, and maybe repeatedly, stops thinking them).

An old New Yorker cartoon showed a worried man at work. Above his desk in a picture frame were the words "Stop thinking." For quite some time, when I would find myself in a repetitious cycle of fearful thoughts,

I would look at this cartoon and stop thinking about the subject(s) that concerned me.

Meditate.

Meditation is another way to stop thinking. Start with a minute or two, and then increase the time to five minutes, then 10, then 15, and longer if you like. What happens slowly, over time, is that you learn to believe in yourself and to have compassion for yourself. This self-confidence and compassion then radiate to your world. If you happen to believe in a God, you will feel more connected to your God. Meditation is a companion to your grief work. It connects you to your deepest self and to your intrinsic worth and power.

Manage insomnia.

Sleep disturbances are normal in grief. You may sleep too little or too much. The disturbances may abate quite naturally over time.

Fear and anger can cause insomnia. You may fall asleep easily only to awaken between 2 and 5 a.m. as fear and frustration may arise and take over.

Clark Strand (2015), who explores spiritual and human issues, describes the time between 2 and 5 a.m. as a wakeful time for many. It is sometimes referred to as "the hour of the wolf" and is characterized by thoughts that are in preparation for our upcoming day or thoughts about our future upcoming days. We have probably all had the experience of waking during that time and trying desperately to get back to sleep only to find ourselves deep in anxiety, plagued by repetitious thoughts about upcoming events. Then, the alarm clock goes off, daylight comes, and the worries recede.

Let's explore two avenues to help your insomnia: using sleep hygiene principles and working with your angry and fearful thoughts when you are experiencing insomnia.

Follow sleep hygiene principles.

To get a good night's sleep, maybe all you need to do is follow sleep hygiene principles (National Center for Chronic Disease Prevention amd Health Promotion, n.d.):

- Go to bed at the same time each night and rise at the same time each morning.
- Make sure your bedroom is a quiet, dark, and relaxing environment, neither too hot nor too cold.
- Make sure your bed is comfortable, and use it only for sleeping and not for other activities, such as reading, watching TV, or listening to music. Remove all TVs, computers, and other "gadgets" from the bedroom.
- Avoid large meals before bedtime.

In addition, using common sense will support your nighttime sleep. If you enjoy physical exercise, do so early in the day. Strenuous exercise near bedtime can cause wakefulness. Limit your caffeine and alcohol intake. Avoid stimulating, fear-producing, and anger-producing conversations at bedtime. If you like to read before bedtime, read something that inspires and relaxes you. Save the murder mystery for daylight hours. Maybe it is not a good idea to watch the 11 o'clock news. Watch the 6 o'clock news instead, giving yourself time to unwind and relax before bedtime.

You can also discuss sleep problems with your doctor or a neurologist who is knowledgeable about "sleep hygiene."

Work with your angry and fearful thoughts when you are experiencing insomnia.

Nighttime emotions frequently recede at daylight. Before then, you can take time to work with them. See this as an opportunity to learn, and to get back to sleep soon. Strand (2010) recommends that if you wake up and are fearful or angry, try the following:

Take out a pen and write your wakeful thoughts in your journal. Take no more than five or ten minutes to do this.

Talk aloud about your angry and fearful thoughts. (This may not be possible if there are other sleepers in your bedroom or house.)

If you can go outside and feel safe doing so, you might consider going outside, because the natural environment can help. Or sit on your porch. Or open a window and feel the early morning air come in and enjoy the sounds of nature. Again, write or speak your thoughts while in or close to nature.

Sit in silence, take some deep breaths and meditate or pray, or read something that gives you inspiration and peace.

Talk about your anger.

Find a friend or a support group to talk with about your angry feelings. Though you may not ask for it or appreciate it, some people will give advice. Some advice can be helpful and may save you from outbursts of anger and confrontations that may prove to be embarrassing and possibly dangerous. (As an example of a dangerous outcome, you could be planning an act of retaliation or revenge). When you take into consideration advice on anger, you may learn another side of the story or a different way of dealing with the situation.

Many people are uncomfortable with anger. To hear you talk about anger may be threatening to some people and their immediate reaction may be to try to fix it, to get you over your anger, to rectify the situation, and even to agree with you. What you need is someone to listen to you. Today, bereavement support groups abound. If the group is properly facilitated and led, you will be listened to, and you will learn how to listen with an open heart and an open mind. Anger can feel justifiable and can be justifiable. Talking about anger can help.

Talk about your fears.

When you talk with others about your fears, they may become uncomfortable and immediately say, "Don't be afraid." "I never felt that way." "You used to be so strong. What happened?" What happened is grief. Fear can be a natural response to change. If you can find a support group or a sympathetic individual to talk to, talking may give you the confidence and the appreciation you deserve as you tackle your fears. You may be afraid that you will get the same illness as your loved one. Finally, you go to the doctor, and find out that you are FINE. You may be afraid of traveling alone, and you take a short trip by yourself. Many people will not notice that these are big accomplishments, but someone who has had losses and fears will appreciate your efforts and may say, "Awesome!"

Write about your anger and fear.

Writing is a powerful tool. It slows down the mind. You may feel that anger and fear have a grip on you, but through writing, you get a grip on them. What are you experiencing that brings up angry and fearful thoughts? Betrayal? Disrespect? Diminishment? Abandonment? Loneliness? Unworthiness? Writing helps you to identify and name your thoughts, and to use your imagination to work with them.

Try not to use your computer. Instead, write by hand in a journal. The time it takes to write longhand helps you to slow down your mind, become calmer, and gain control of your anger and fears. Author Julie Cameron (1992) recommends a form of writing that she calls The Morning Pages. As soon as you awaken in the morning, take up your journal, and write three pages. If you can't think of anything to write, you can start with "I can't think of anything to write." Simply keep writing. It can seem like a stream of consciousness. Slowly you may be writing about your anger and fears. Cameron's book, *The Artist's Way*, is written for artists who want to overcome a block to be more creative and productive. You too are an artist. You are an artist of your grief.

Act on your justifiable anger in a constructive way.

If your loved one died violently (a homicide or a suicide, a terrorist act, a car accident), you may find it helpful to channel your anger into ways that help you to understand your loved one's death: to right the wrong of the death through advocacy groups or through the judicial system; to provide support to other survivors through sharing your own experience.

If you are considering revenge or personal retaliation, these acts will only add to the suffering that has already occurred, and it is imperative that you seek counseling.

Weep.

Anger and fear are heavy burdens to carry. When this burden gets heavier and heavier, you may find that one day, you just sit down and cry. And suddenly the anger and fear dissipate or get less burdensome. If you feel stuck and cannot cry but would like to cry, listen to music or watch a movie that touches you.

A note about weeping: just because you are not weeping does not mean that you are not grieving. Weeping is not required. Remember that your grief is unique to you. Grief will happen with or without weeping.

Exercise.

Exercise is good for every organ of your body, including your brain. Your thoughts originate in the brain, and then from these thoughts come emotions, such as anger and fear. Exercise helps to dissipate and lessen these thoughts and emotions. When you are in distress, exercise may be beneficial. Swimming can be both an aerobic exercise and therapeutic at the same time. Water can have a calming effect on your body and mind. If you like exercise, try mixing it up. If you exercise at a gym, instead go outside for a walk or a run. At the end of your outdoor or indoor exercise, consciously slow down and appreciate your inner state.

Work physically.

Chop wood, garden, shovel snow, rake leaves. Not only do these tasks take a lot of energy, they are creative. You have created something whether it is wood for your fireplace, a clean sidewalk, or a tidy garden. This is satisfying.

Breathe.

Breathe deeply. Take in a long slow breath, counting as you breathe in. When you exhale, add a count. If you inhale to the count of 4, exhale to the count of 5. Do this several times. Then, simply breathe and become aware of the calm repetitive nature of your breath. Relish its rhythm and peacefulness.

Touch.

Anger and fear separate us from each other and from ourselves. If you feel comfortable, ask for a hug from a friend. Or ask permission to give a hug. Human touch helps us to feel oneness and a sense of belonging.

To connect with yourself, put your hands on your chest in the area of your heart. Hold them there gently for a few minutes. Feel the heat of your hands on your heart and enjoy this healing touch.

Engage with nature. Befriend nature.

Spiritual teacher, Eckhart Tolle, says "Everything natural—every flower, tree, and animal—has important lessons to teach us if we only stop, look, and listen" (2009, p. 30). Nature has a way of giving us messages. You can silently ask the question, "What can I learn from you? What message is here for me?"

- Being in the presence of tall majestic trees can give you a sense of safety.
- Seeing a sapling can give you hope.
- Seeing colorful flowers, from the common dandelion to the majestic rose, can give you the feeling of mutual love and oneness.
- Gazing at the sky can give you a feeling of freedom.
- Inhaling crisp morning air can give you enthusiasm and energy.
- Seeing the stars at night can make you quiet and humble.
- Watching a flower bloom on your stubborn houseplant can give you joy.
- On a day when you can't get moving, seeing and hearing busy birds outside your window can get you on your way.

Nature is a great sage.

Invite fear along.

A meditation monk shared the following approach with me and has given me permission to share it with you. Fear can be overwhelming, for example, when one is going to speak publicly or travel alone. Invite fear along: "Fear, you have been with me for a long time, and we have had many confrontations and conversations. You can come along with me and be at my side as my old companion. But I am in charge today." You have removed fear as an adversary who takes a lot of energy to fight and reason with. Now, fear is by your side, and you are okay. Fighting fear can reinforce it! By giving up the fight, you leave room for winning freedom.

Two weeks after 9/11, I was scheduled to take a flight to Texas on American Airlines, one of the airlines whose plane was hijacked. At that time, there was a lot of fear in my community of Washington, DC. F-16 fighter planes were flying overhead day and night. The news was full of 9/11 reports. Many people decided to leave the Washington, DC, area permanently for safety. I felt my fears were justified. For the two weeks prior to the flight, I meditated and journaled on a regular basis. On the day of the flight, I invited my fear along as an old friend. After all, it had its point. As I boarded the plane, I felt calm and focused, immediately followed by powerful love and compassion for my fellow travelers, the airline personnel, and all who had died on 9/11.

The lights in the plane were on. The passengers, though obviously mindful of the situation, were laughing and talking together. The airline staff was sensitive and kind, and they expressed gratitude that we were flying with American. We were love warriors. For that day, fear had lost its power.

Say thank-you.

When you are angry or afraid, simply say these two words: thank-you. You may be amazed what comes up for you. Gratitude is a way to see the bigger, better picture and to attune you to more than what you may be experiencing at the moment.

Seek help and guidance.

Your angry and fearful thoughts may be so intense and severe that you need outside or professional help in managing them. See the tables below for when to get help.

When to get help with your anger

You have suicidal and/or homicidal thoughts and especially if you have a plan as to how to complete your suicide or a homicide.

You frequently lash out emotionally or physically at others.

You find you are angry most of the time, over many different things. This can be a sign of a clinical depression, where anger can be a constant undercurrent.

Nothing pleases you. You experience that there is something wrong with everything. You frequently say "yes, but..." when someone presents an alternative view.

You engage in risky behaviors to subdue your feelings, such as abusing alcohol or drugs.

> **When to get help with your fear**
>
> You are experiencing anxiety attacks such that it is hard to function.
>
> You have symptoms of Post-Traumatic Stress Disorder (PTSD). See Chapter 11.
>
> You constantly ruminate about your fears: you find yourself thinking the same fearful thoughts over and over. You find that you cannot break this cycle.
>
> You frequently experience dread and a sense of doom. This can be a sign of depression.
>
> You think about suicide and especially if you have a plan as to how you will complete it.

Chapter Summary

Anger and fear are normal (and ancient) emotions that we all have. At times, they may seem like enemies. You wonder, "Why does every little thing seem to bother me?" "I wish I were brave." Instead, see them as signals that something disturbing to you has happened, something important to you has been violated, or something has changed in your life to make you sad—and sometimes afraid and angry, too.

Anger and fear separate us from one another, and they diminish our inner sense of well-being. We may feel powerless.

There are ways to work with your anger and your fear. Some of these ways take on the emotion directly: thinking, using your imagination to find alternatives to your anger and fear, talking, writing, weeping, expressing justifiable anger, seeking professional help. Other ways support you more generally but are equally important: exercising, using your body to work (gardening, shoveling snow), deep breathing, meditating, stopping thoughts, using sleep hygiene principles, engaging with nature, reaching out to others, and saying "thank-you."

Chapter 6

Task 2: To Experience the Pain of Grief— Experiencing the Pain of Guilt and Shame

> *"Its (guilt) cultivation in people—along with shame—serves the noblest, most generous and humane character traits that distinguishes our species."*
> —*Willard Gaylin, psychiatrist, medical ethicist*

In this chapter, I will explore two very uncomfortable experiences: guilt and shame. They reveal to us, not always accurately, that we have done something wrong, and they manifest in different ways.

Overview of guilt and shame

Elisabeth Kübler-Ross said, "Guilt is perhaps the most painful companion of death" (1969, p.169). Guilt is painful. Shame is painful. They are also important and a necessary part of humanity. These emotions reach to our collective human conscience; they challenge us to do better so that we can learn from our mistakes and participate more fully in our society; they help to keep our society together and challenge us to examine our society. They address the state we are all in as we participate in life. None of us is perfect. We are all going to make mistakes. Guilt and shame help us to contemplate our mistakes and rectify them. If we did not have these emotions, our society would not function.

Guilt and shame teach us that we can do better. Guilt appears between the ages of three and six years of age. Shame appears between the ages of 14 and 16 months. Both occur in all cultures and have similarities and differences. In more individualistic or heterogeneous cultures, guilt predominates. In more group-oriented or homogeneous cultures, shame predominates (Stadter, 2012).

If I do something that I judge to be wrong, I can experience guilt, shame, or both. With guilt, I judge my behavior. There is the possibility of change—I have the power to change my behavior. With shame, I judge myself as being bad and do not have the possibility of change. I feel powerless. I expect the judgment, rejection, and recrimination from others. I may want to simply disappear, lash out in anger, and may even show physical symptoms such as blushing and lowering of the eyes.

These emotions remind us, very uncomfortably, that it is impossible to be perfect. We are imperfect. In grief, we may imagine that we are more imperfect than we really are because we do not get a chance to say we are sorry, to make things right, or to do something different.

Using the models of Lewis (1971) and Tangney and Dearing (2002), Michael Stadter (2012), a clinical psychologist, has described the similarities and differences between guilt and shame. Table 6.1 illustrates these two emotions. The antidote to guilt is forgiveness. The antidote to shame is connection to others and to oneself.

Guilt is a powerful motivator for change. If I do something wrong, I can make amends and change my behavior for the better. I can forgive the mistakes of my past. I am powerful.

In shame, self-recrimination reigns, and change feels out of the question. I feel powerless.

Let's look at each and how they might manifest in grieving.

Experiencing the pain of guilt

In human relationships, we have a mixture of negative and positive feelings about those we love. No matter how careful we try to be, when we love someone deeply for a long time, we will inevitably hurt and be hurt by that person. Especially in stressful times, one's best self may not always come forward.

When death occurs, the painful feelings of guilt can arise because there is no way to take hurtful thoughts or actions back. Guilt is a frequent and normal feeling in grief. If you find yourself saying, "I wish I had…," "If only…," or "I should have…," you are experiencing guilt.

Table 6.1
The differences and similarities between guilt and shame

Guilt	Shame
I feel bad about doing something wrong.	I am bad.
The person has the need to confess.	The person has the need to disappear.
Guilt targets the behaviour. I did something bad.	Shame targets the person. I am bad.
Guilt motivates us to do better.	Shame makes us feel we cannot do better.
Guilt may only be visible to the guilty person; it is an interior, private response.	Shame is visible to others: the person may blush, exit the situation, shut down, or get angry.
Origin can be interior.	Origin can be from others: "Aren't you over this?" Or "I never felt that way."
The person feels powerful.	The person feels powerless (humiliated, embarrassed).
We ridicule ourselves.	We expect the scorn and ridicule of others. We may also ridicule (shame) others.
Antidote to guilt: forgiveness.	Antidote to shame: connection to others and oneself – self-acceptance. Take the risk and reach out to others.

Survivors may feel guilty about

- not knowing enough;
- not doing enough;
- choosing the wrong treatment;
- choosing the wrong doctor;
- saying the wrong things;
- not being there at the right time;
- ambivalent feelings about the deceased; and/or
- wishing for the end of a long illness.

In the early part of grief, the grieving person tends to be hard on himself, sometimes feeling that if he had done something differently, his loved one would still be alive (Rando, 1991).

Then there are times where your actions or inactions contributed to the person's discomfort, harm, or even death; when there were things you could have said that would have cemented the relationship or cleared the air; and/or when you neglected to do things that could have been helpful.

Those who are left behind sometimes feel, "Why did I survive? Others are so much more worthy of life than me." Particularly in sudden, traumatic, or military loss, survivors may struggle with this kind of guilt.

Survivors of loved ones who committed suicide have many painful feelings, including guilt. They may feel at fault for their loved one's death. "If only I had…."

It is important for survivors to seek professional help or a support group should guilty feelings become overwhelming. Others may blame the survivors or may be experiencing their own guilt and be uncomfortable talking with you. You may feel judged and isolated, with no one to talk to.

How to go beyond guilt

In Chapter 5, I discussed managing anger and fear. In this chapter, rather than "managing" guilt, the following ideas are here to encourage you to go beyond it to a more comfortable place of forgiveness, acceptance, and freedom.

Talk about it.

I once heard of a Native American ritual where one enters the sacred tent and tells the Shaman his deepest, darkest secret, something that he has told no one else in the world. The Shaman listens. The effect is to unburden the soul and free the person. To share with another human being what you feel guilty of helps you to identify and confess the guilt, to let it go, and to become whole. First, you must tell the story. Unlike the Shaman, the well-meaning listener may say, "Don't feel guilty." "You did all that you could." "It was out of your hands." Although this kind of reassurance is loving and important, in the beginning, being heard may be most helpful.

Write about it.

To only think about your guilt may get you into the repetitious cycle of thinking the same thing over and over. Writing helps to slow down the repetitious thoughts and gives you some perspective.

To help you get started, complete one or all these sentences. Write without censure.

Guilt Exercise

If only I....

I should have....

I wish I had....

I wish I had not....

It is my fault that....

I feel guilty because I....

Write a letter to your deceased loved one.

In your letter, you can express the guilty thoughts and feelings that you have. Write without reserve. Ask for forgiveness.

Compose a letter from your loved one to you. What would your loved one say to you about the guilt that you are experiencing? [4]

Apply a tincture of time.

Early in grief, you may experience an inordinate amount of guilt, and may berate yourself for all you felt you did wrong, while at the same time idealizing the person who died. As humorist Art Buchwald aptly put it, "When we grieve, tears and guilt get mixed together" (1994, p. 14). As best you can, acknowledge the guilt you are experiencing, write about it, talk about it, and then let some time elapse, maybe a year. Then, revisit your guilt. You may find that your guilt feelings are not so strong, and that your idealized feelings about your loved one are more realistic.

Forgive yourself.

Harold Ivan Smith, grief specialist, says, "Forgiveness is a decision we keep making. Forgiveness is 'for giving.' It releases us from the exhausting work of lugging around a grudge like homeless people carrying their belongings" (2007, p. 74). In guilt, the grudge is against yourself. He tells us

---
[4] These are techniques suggested by Neimeyer (2012).

that the prefix "for" points toward the goal of "giving." Who are you giving to? What are you giving? You are giving yourself the gifts of freedom and compassion.

Create a forgiveness ritual.

Prayer of forgiveness.

Reverend Granger Westberg recommends Psalm 51 Verses 1 and 10, as a beautiful prayer asking for forgiveness, "Have mercy on me, oh God. Create in me a clean heart, oh God, and renew a right spirit within me" (2011, p. 44). You can also recite another prayer or create your own prayer.

Daily practice

Charles Fillmore (1969), the 19th and early 20th century religious leader and co-founder of Unity, an interdenominational spiritual community, had a simple forgiveness ritual: Every night as you are lying in bed, waiting for sleep, bring forth everyone who has slighted or wronged you, and say, "I forgive you." Then forgive yourself, "I forgive myself." That's it. The world is filled with past wrongs that cannot or will not be righted. Forgive everyone of everything. Fillmore does not say, forget. He only says forgive. You don't have to forget. You just have to forgive.

Visualization

Visualize the person from whom you are seeking forgiveness. Before you do this, take a few deep breaths so that you feel relaxed and present. Close your eyes. In your imagination, face the person, and ask their forgiveness. Wait a few minutes, and rest here. You may feel an inner shift in your state, as well as a change in the person from whom you are seeking forgiveness. How can you not be forgiven? When you ask for forgiveness in this way, it is always granted. You are choosing forgiveness. Really, forgiveness is for you. It is as natural as breathing. It is a gift of love to yourself and to others. You may possibly weep with sorrow, remorse, or regret. That's okay. These are tears of love. Take another few deep breaths, and open your eyes.

Make amends in the present. Move it forward.

In the present, choose behavior that is different. The past is over, and there is no way for you to go back and make it better. Take in the knowledge that you have learned with a humble heart. Now you know. Now you understand. You can move forward and make your life and the lives of others better. For example:

> If you wished the ordeal of caring for your loved one would end quickly, be patient and accepting in the face of future caregiving events.
>
> If you knew that your loved one was dying, and at the same time didn't know it (this is called middle knowledge), in the future, try to be diligent and not get into the trap of middle knowledge. (See Chapter 3).
>
> If you were angry and judgmental of your loved one, practice kindness in your present relationships.
>
> If you were impatient with your loved one, try offering work (paid or volunteer) with a population that is similar to your loved one, e.g., a youth group, or the elderly.

These are ways of making amends in the present for past behaviors. These are ways of moving it forward. When you move it forward, you are changing the focus from your mind (which is thinking judgmental and guilt-filled thoughts) to your remorseful heart (which is inspiring you to move toward positive, helpful actions). Guilt is in the mind. Remorse is in the heart. Guilt is a judgment. Remorse is sorrow about what you have done.

Choose to be free.

You can choose not to think guilty thoughts: those thoughts that you have gone over in your mind thousands of times, thoughts that come up when there is a reminder—maybe a room you enter or a street you cross. One day, you can choose: I am sorry for what I did, or for how I acted, or for what I said, or for what I did not know. Today, I am not going to think about it. I am going to enjoy this moment, this day.

Of all the painful emotions, guilt is an acceptable human emotion. We can function while experiencing guilt, and maybe that's why it can linger and continue to crop up even when we think we have left it behind.

Julie Potter, MSW, LCSW

Experiencing the pain of shame

Shame is a partner of guilt. It is caused by a strong sense of guilt, embarrassment, unworthiness, or disgrace. It comes from the word "to cover."[5]

You may experience shame that you are not grieving well, fast enough, or at all. Sometimes, the comments of well-meaning people can make you feel shame, e.g., "I'm worried about you. You seem so sad all the time. You are not yourself. I miss the 'old you.'" Should I be happy? Who exactly am I now? Why can't I be the "old you"?

Shame can be experienced in support groups and in individual therapy sessions. It may seem to you that members in the group may be "progressing" faster than you are. A therapist can subtly convey disappointment in your progress, or you may feel shame that you are stuck.

Linda Hartling (2000), PhD, clinical/community psychologist, describes three common ways that people might deal with shame:

Move away. The shamed person can hide, withdraw, shut down, and keep the shamed feeling a secret.

Move toward. The shamed person seeks to please and appease those with whom she feels shame.

Move against. The shamed person tries to gain power over others, by being aggressive and by using shame to fight shame. One uses aggression to hide one's shame. You might fight back by saying, "You don't understand," "You are insensitive," "You have worse faults than I have," etc. These strategies may work in the short run.

All three of these methods may mask or hide shame, but they also disconnect us from others. We are hiding our self from others at a time when connection to others is healing and important.

Shame is associated with self-esteem. You have lost your loved one and significant identities. These identities enhanced your self-esteem: spouse, child, sibling, caregiver, "chief cook and bottle washer." Now that your loved one is gone, it is normal to feel "out of it," not knowing what to do, no longer fitting in and feeling a part of the scheme of things.

---

5   Here is the etymology of the word, *shame*, as far as linguists can track its evolution, beginning with the Proto-Indo-European (PIE—the language that predates by far English and a number of other related languages) word, *kem (to cover, as in to cover oneself), evolving, with a typical consonant shift, into PIE *skem, then with another regular consonant and vowel shift, appearing as *scamu* in Old English and, with some pronunciation changes as *shame* in modern English.

The pain of shame and a low self-esteem can temporarily accompany other life changes whether they are positive or negative: marriage, a new job, being laid off or fired from a job, retirement, disabilities, and illnesses.

How to go beyond shame

As stated in the beginning, shame is a natural human emotion. We can go beyond it in one instance, and then it may appear again. Each appearance of shame is an opportunity for inner growth. The following are ways to go beyond shame.

Connect with others and with yourself.

Shame disconnects you from others and from yourself. Although your experience is shame, remember that others have their own agenda and may not even notice your perceived shortcomings. Talk with a trusted friend about how you feel. You may find that others share your feelings or are sympathetic, or it may be a revelation to them of how you are feeling. Reaching out to others helps them, too, because you are sharing your humanity with them, that is, your imperfection. Yes, this takes courage. It is at these times that it is important to reconnect with yourself and remind yourself that you are a unique and worthwhile human being in spite of the shameful feelings that may arise.

Be imperfect.

It is perfect to be imperfect. Give yourself permission to make mistakes as you learn new skills, as you grieve at your own pace, as you create a new you. All times are times to be imperfect. We cannot always get it right. We make mistakes. We hurt others. We put our foot in our mouth. This is all part of being a person.

Don Coyhis, Mohican Nation leader and author, talks about mistakes this way:

> The Creator designed us to learn by trial and error (participation). The path of life we walk is very wide. Everything on the path is sacred. What we do right is sacred but our mistakes are also sacred. This is the Creator's way of teaching spiritual people. To criticise ourselves when we make mistakes is not the Indian way. To learn from our mistakes is the Indian way. The definition of a spiritual person is someone who makes thirty to fifty mistakes

each day and talks to the Creator after each one to see what to do next time. This is the way of the spiritual warrior (cited by Schaef, 1995, p. 107).

Just as you are compassionate and forgiving of others and find yourself suspending judgment of them, it is a good idea to extend this same compassion and forgiveness to yourself and to suspend judgment of yourself.

See your journey through life as a path, with many successes, failures, and near misses. Every so often, look back over your path, and you will see that even though there are scraggly parts, there is also beauty. You are creating your path in your own way. Many uncomfortable emotions, like guilt and shame, will crop up. These emotions are present in your journey; they are not there to hold you back; they are guideposts on your journey. You can make the decision now, before your journey is complete: you are forgiven. Case dismissed.

Be prepared to dismiss your case many times. In your own private court of law, the case may come up again and again. Don't argue with yourself when this happens. Hear the evidence with compassion. And then, remember: no appeals. Case dismissed.

Feelings of grief that pop up out of the blue, for the rest of our lives, are called STUGs (Subsequent Temporary Upsurges of Grief) (Rando, 1993). Guilt and shame may also appear unexpectedly.

Throughout your life, even if you have put instances of guilt and shame to rest, even if you have forgiven yourself, and even if you have made amends, be prepared for them to pop up. Accept them with love, and then let them go.

When emotions of guilt and shame remain unresolved, it may be time to seek help.

> **When to Get Help**
>
> If guilt is long-standing, and you just can't shake it, it may inhibit your development as a human being.
>
> If shame is long-standing, and you just can't shake it, it may further compromise your self-esteem and may be a sign of depression.

Chapter Summary

Guilt and shame are two emotions that help to maintain and preserve one's society and social group. Without them, society would be in chaos.

Guilt gives power to the person. You judge your behavior as bad, and you have the power to change your behavior.

Shame diminishes your power. You judge yourself as being bad because of your behavior. When you are shamed, you may want to disappear, to seek to please the one who shamed you, or to cause the other person to feel shame. Connecting with yourself and with others gives relief.

In grief, guilt and shame are particularly painful because there is no going back for a second chance to get it right. Death puts a stop to second chances. Even the smallest transgression can be magnified: I didn't get there in time. I was annoyed with her. I was unkind to him. I didn't tell her I loved her. In grief, all transgressions feel big. We wish we could have been perfect and gotten everything right. But, by our nature, we are imperfect. We get some things right, but we don't get everything right. We don't get a dress rehearsal for life or death. We learn as we go along. We make it up as we go along. We try hard. We are there at just the right moment. We are not there at the important moment. Sometimes, we phone it in.

It is good to work through what you may feel guilty of and what you may be ashamed of. It helps to talk with someone who will listen, to write a letter to your loved one, to write a letter as if it were from your loved one, to write about your thoughts and feelings, to be gentle with yourself at a time when all you may feel is harshness toward yourself, and to give yourself time and revisit your guilt or shame in a year.

Forgive yourself, and connect with others. Although it is too late to make amends to your loved one, you can choose different behavior in the present. If you were unkind, you can choose kindness now. If you were annoyed, you can be patient now. If you were not there at the most precious moment, you can be there for others in their precious moments. If you didn't say you loved him, you can say it now and often to others whom you love.

We are all in the same boat of life. Forgiving yourself, forgiving others, and connecting with others helps you on your journey. It helps others in their life journey, too. As you are making progress with these emotions, you are learning and contributing to your society.

Chapter 7

Task 2: To Experience the Pain of Grief— Experiencing the Pain of Sadness and Depression

"Some of you say, 'Joy is greater than sorrow' and others say 'Nay, sorrow is the greater.' But I say unto you, 'They are inseparable.'"
—*Kahlil Gibran,* **The Prophet**

"Even in laughter the heart is sorrowful, and the end of mirth is sadness."
—*Proverbs 14:13*

Sadness is normal in grief. In this chapter, I will discuss sadness and the important differences between grief-related sadness and clinical depression.

Sadness vs. depression

My daughter loved her grandparents, who lived out of town. At the end of one visit, as we were driving away, I turned around to look out the rear-view window for one last look at Mom and Dad waving good-bye to us. Gail, who was six years old, was in the back seat, and she, too, was looking out the rear-window. She was sobbing and waving at the same time. Sadness. Sadness is a heartfelt feeling. The sad feelings and thoughts that you experience are an expression of your love.

In grief, sadness is heartrending because the loss is permanent.

Sadness may not be immediately experienced on a conscious level. So many other things are going on at the same time:

- the shock of the loss;
- the need to make immediate and practical decisions;
- guilt and regrets about missed opportunities;
- anger at those who may have caused the loss (a negligent automobile driver, an illness or injury, the medical profession, oneself, God or nature, or the deceased who may not have "taken care" of herself);
- relief that it is over and a sense of freedom;
- fears about the present: "What do I do now?"
- fears about future: "Will I be okay?" "Can I take care of myself?"
- broken dreams;
- free-floating fear and anxiety;
- loneliness;
- longing for the past; and
- trying to forget the past or reconcile with the past and forgive.

Underlying all of this may be sadness in its purest "I miss you" form, with accompanying thoughts, feelings, and tears. In fact, all the above is a part of sadness or right next door to it.

Sometimes, deep sadness will trigger a clinical depression. The sadness experienced in grief and in clinical depression has similarities, with an important difference. In grief, the sadness is related to the loss. In clinical depression, the sad feelings are generalized to all of life.

Aaron Beck (2009), MD, a psychiatrist, who is considered the father of Cognitive Therapy, says that the clinically depressed person has three modes of thinking. He has:

- a negative view of the world
- a negative view of self
- a negative view of the future.

Further, the clinically depressed person feels

- very sad
- hopeless
- unimportant and
- unable to live in a normal way.

In grief, you may temporarily experience these same modes of thinking and feeling. Let's look at the characteristics of clinical depression and how they manifest temporarily in grief.

The grieving person experiences sadness and may have one or more kinds of negative views.

A negative view of the world in grief
Your personal world and the world in general, may seem dark, empty, and sad without your loved one.

A negative view of self in grief
You may experience a low self-esteem because your roles in life as spouse, parent, friend, or caregiver have ended. Your life may have lost its meaning. "My confidence is gone. Who am I? I used to be able to do so much. Now I feel I can do nothing."

A negative view of the future in grief
"I had hopes and plans for the future. That future is gone. My life is a broken dream."

The grieving person may feel grief through a variety of emotions.

Very sad in grief
Tears may come easily and at unexpected times. There may be a sense of longing and pining for the deceased.

Hopeless in grief
"If I died today, I wouldn't feel bad at all. My life is over." Grieving people may experience this feeling temporarily. It is a normal part of grief. When it is all pervasive, and there is no relief from this idea, or one makes plans to end one's life, then it is time to get help.

Unimportant in grief
A component of grief is low self-esteem—the feeling of being unimportant and unnecessary. With life's changes, whether good or bad, our identity and roles change. Although you may be able to do new things, you cannot always do what you used to do. You may feel unimportant and experience a temporary challenge to your self-esteem as you adjust to life's changes and learn new skills.

Unable to live in a normal way in grief
Your normal way of living has changed, and you have to start from scratch creating a new normal way of living.

Grief-related sadness is temporary. Clinical depression is longstanding and chronic.

Table 7.1, created by Alan Wolfelt (1988), PhD, author and grief counselor, shows differences between normal grief sadness and clinical depression. If you think you may have a clinical depression, you may worry that if you get treatment for depression it will take away your grief and appreciation for your loved one. Treatment will not take away your grief, but it will help you to function better and feel better than you are feeling.

Table 7.1
Possible distinctions between normal grief sadness and clinical depression

Normal grief sadness	Clinical depression
Responds to comfort and support.	Does not accept support.
Often openly angry.	Irritable and may complain but does not directly express anger.
Relates depressed feelings to loss experienced.	Does not relate experiences to a particular life event.
Can still experience moments of enjoyment in life.	Exhibits an all-pervading sense of doom.
Exhibits feelings of sadness and emptiness.	Projects a sense of hopelessness and chronic emptiness.
May have transient physical complaints.	Has chronic physical complaints.
Expresses guilt over some specific aspect of the loss.	Has generalised feelings of guilt.
Has temporary impact upon self-esteem.	Loss of self-esteem is of longer duration.

How to help your sadness

Treasure your sadness.

Sadness is a part of love. Since we are finite, we will eventually lose all the people and all the things that we love. Sadness is your expression of love for that which you have lost. At times, you may feel engulfed in sadness, without any effort on your part. It simply happens, and you may find yourself thinking, feeling, and weeping at completely unexpected times.

Give a form to your sadness.

Funerals and memorial events give form to sadness in the company of your community. When you give form to your sadness, you are using your power to contain it. Sadness does not go away in these rituals; it is contained and expressed within the ritual.

Anniversary events—recurring significant events such as holidays and birthdays—are times when you can plan specific activities and remembrance rituals to honor the day. Many people find it helpful to plan for these events, rather than being caught off-guard when they happen. (See more about anniversary suggestions in Chapter 9.)

Talk and write about your sad and depressed feelings.

Sadness is a signal to you that something precious in your life has ended or changed. Talk about how you feel with someone who will be present with you and who will not give a lot of advice. Write in your journal what you are thinking and feeling, especially when sadness is intense.

Many people benefit from a guided journaling process. One such method is the Progoff Intensive Journal Method, created by Ira Progoff. Progoff, a psychotherapist, studied how famous historical figures developed fulfilling lives. With this knowledge, he helped his clients to overcome their problems and lead meaningful lives. He found that clients progressed more rapidly when they wrote in a journal. Consequently, he created the Progoff Intensive Journal Method. One can learn the method from his book, *At a Journal Workshop,* and/or attend a workshop. For more about the method, visit Intensivejournal.org.

A participant writes about her experience with the Intensive Journal method:

For many years, I have used the Intensive Journal method as a guide out of the darkest places of pain, no matter how lost I feel. The structure of the method consistently offers me a centering place in which to work through loss, sort out feelings, and seek positive change in my life. Through the process, I can reach the deepest places of grief when I am ready, look into the darkest corners at soul level, and then take healing steps toward a healthy and full life once again.

—Pam Rivers (from Intensive Journal website)

Read a poem. Write a poem.

Jack Leedy, a poetry therapist, had this to say about the healing power of a poem: "Take two aspirin and one poem," and "Take a poem, not a pill" (cited by Reiter, 2004, p. 231). During World War II, many people who were in concentration camps wrote poetry. It helped them to put their experience into rhythmic words. When the war ended, and those who survived returned to normal life, most of them never wrote poetry again.

Charles Crootof (1969), psychoanalyst, tells us:

"The extent to which poetry has provided solace and comfort to humanity through the ages is buried in the history of mankind. We will never know how many hearts and minds have been stirred to feel less alienated and more human by the quiet beauty of 'The Song of Solomon,' by the tragic suffering of a Job or an Oedipus, or by the derring-do of a Beowulf" (p. 39).

Have a book of poetry by your bedside, on your coffee table, or in your office for a pick-me-up. Below is a list of some poetry anthologies and books that you may find helpful.

Poetry suggestions

The Art of Losing: Poems of Grief and Healing, by Kevin Young

Good Poems for Hard Times, editor, Garrison Keillor

Good Poems, editor, Garrison Keillor

Horoscopes for the Dead, Billy Collins

The New Yorker Book of Poems, selected by the editors of the New Yorker

The New Oxford Book of English Verse, editor, Helen Gardner

The Oxford Book of American Poetry, editors, David Lehman, John Brehm

The Prophet, by Kahlil Gibran

A Rumor of Angels, editor, Gail Perry Johnston

The Soul of the World, editor, Phil Cousineau, photographs, Eric Lawton

The Psalms from the Old Testament

Listen to Music. Create Music.

Music touches our heartstrings and unites the mind with the heart. Singer-songwriter Neko Case suffered from depression and found that at one point in her life she could not sing or write music anymore. She didn't even like the sound of music!

> And that's one of the ways I knew something was really wrong with me. I just found lyrics...grating and so I started listening to ragtime and I found that that was really comforting. It was like a little bubbling engine. It was like a little teapot—the old style like my grandma had. Like the percolator which was always like the good coffee smell in the morning. Like, 'All right we're getting going. Everything's going to be great.' So, that's kind of how it felt (Case, 2013, n.p.).

Ragtime helped her to get back to singing and writing again.

Music can bring back painful memories but can also help you transcend them. Find music that you enjoy: classical, rock-and-roll, marches, religious music, show music, the blues?

Do something or create something in memory of your loved one.

Every year, I write a check to two hospices, one in whose care my sister died and one in whose care my brother died. It gives me deep pleasure to see their names in print as I fill out the hospice donation forms, and it brings back memories of the special times we had together. I want to support the important work of hospice, and sending a donation helps me to stay connected with my brother and sister.

My sister founded a community art gallery called Art Upstairs in Morristown, New Jersey, in an old movie theatre that was renovated to be a community center for the lively arts. She managed the exhibitions, and she enjoyed her work. After she died, my brother-in-law initiated and participated in a project to display her artwork in the gallery, along with the work of many artists she had helped. Family, friends, and members of the community came together to celebrate her life and her work. A special plaque in her memory now hangs in the gallery. It was a wonderful way to celebrate her life and her contribution to her community. We were sad and happy at the same time—sad that she was gone, happy to remember.

Take a break from your sadness.

Remove or rearrange reminders. You may experience that thinking, feeling, and weeping are happening too much. Too hard to look at that empty chair? Try sitting in it so you don't see it. Is the quiet too intense? Watch the news or listen to the radio at mealtimes. Is the empty spot in the bed too big? Sleep on your partner's side of the bed or pile up a lot of pillows next to you, or sleep in a different room for a while.

A widow relates her way of taking a break from sadness:

After my husband died, every time I looked at his picture, I broke down and cried. And there were a lot of his pictures in the house. So, I turned all the pictures of him around so that I wouldn't see his likeness. I simply was just too sad. As the weeks and months went on, little by little, and one by one, I turned the pictures back.

Set a specific time to be sad.

Allot a half-hour or an hour daily or weekly when you can think about, cry about, and/or write about all that you have lost. This may be unrealistic in the beginning, but as time goes on, this can give you a sense of control and some relief from sadness.

Find rhythm. Create rhythm.

Why is it that the sun rising every day and setting every night is so beautiful to behold? It can take our breath away. Why is it that the moon's predictable phases inspire us? Why is it that the repetitious waves on the shore can have a calming effect on us? Rhythm.

These predictable rhythms are monotonous and repetitious but not boring. You never hear someone say, "Oh no, there goes the sun again." or "Is that all there is to the moon?" or "Okay, I get it. One wave after the other." These are the rhythms of life, the rhythms of nature, that give us solace and peace. Mohandas Gandhi said, "Monotony is the law of nature. Look at the monotonous manner in which the sun rises. The monotony of necessary occupation is exhilarating and life giving" (cited in Duncan, 2005, p. 246).

Some would say that rhythm is life. Rocking, being held next to the heart comforts a baby. Listening to songs and hearing bedtime stories encourages slumber.

When you go to work, you are following a schedule. This can give you comfort even if you think your job is not the greatest.

When you are in a state of upheaval, the dependable rhythms of life are disrupted. Your habitual way of living and your habits of the heart have changed. Phone calls, visits, special shared events, the electronic buzz of emails, texts, tweets, Facebook—these are a few of the dependable rhythms of relationships that change when a death occurs.

Appreciate the rhythms in your life and start to create new rhythms—maybe a daily walk. Try to get up at the same time every day. Go to bed at the same time every night. Eat at the same times for meals.

Being out of rhythm can also be healing.

You may need that extra two hours of sleep every day. You may need naps. You may need to sit and stare and do nothing. Your appetite may be kaput, and the last thing you want to do is eat a morsel of food. You may find yourself snacking rather than sitting down to a meal. Just notice the rhythms that you are able to maintain and the rhythms that you are able to create and appreciate yourself for this.

Trust the process, too. Sometimes people work hard to feel better, using a lot of energy. When they don't get results, they may feel discouraged. Trust that you are a part of nature. After a big storm, it takes time for the earth to regenerate, or for the ocean to settle, and re-establish a steady rhythm. When you experience a loss, it takes time for your body and mind to adjust, to heal, and to move forward. Slowly you will be able to experience your life's rhythms. And you may create others.

A man relates a story about how he was living in a chaotic way after his wife died and how he created rhythm in his life:

> Shortly after my wife Charlotte died, I moved into a tiny apartment. It was so small that sometimes, I referred to it as "my cell." But it was perfect for a blind man. I never got lost, and everything I needed was generally within my reach. No frills here, just the bare essentials, which did not include any major cleaning items. And quite frankly, I did not care. I walked through my pain, anger, sadness and depression in far less than a sterile environment. However, I did on occasion, get down on my hands and knees, and scoop up the obvious dust balls. As I think of it now, I'm sure that it had my dear German mother spinning in her grave. She came from the school of "Cleanliness is next to Godliness."

> This lifestyle continued for the better part of one year. It ended abruptly one day, when I was out with a friend who had a number of errands to run. When they were completed, she asked me if there was anything I needed or wanted before she dropped me off at my apartment. I suddenly heard myself saying, "I really, really need a vacuum cleaner." That day we bought a vacuum cleaner and several other cleaning items, including Windex. It was not long after that particular purchase that I overheard people in the building, saying, "Did you hear about the blind man on the 18th floor? I understand he washes windows."

> For me, it was buying a vacuum cleaner, and for a friend, it was when she bought herself a Mickey Mouse watch. Whatever form

it may take, there hopefully comes a time when we feel and sense life's energy returning, a time when we know that if we keep walking eventually we'll see the light at the end of the tunnel. To be sure, it is not always easy, and there can be many obstacles in our way. But, from personal experience, I can assure you that it is well worth the effort.

—Harry Woehrle

Meditate.

Meditation helps the scattered and "arrhythmic" mind to return to its natural rhythm of peace and unity. Meditation is a way to find inner peace and to carry this peace throughout the day. If you find that the only peace you get is when you are meditating, that is fine. More than likely your first efforts at meditation will make you keenly aware of how active your mind is. (Even long-term meditators report periods of meditation that are filled with words, thoughts, and anxieties). This may be discouraging, but see it as a good sign. You are in a space of quiet, and now the loudest being in the room is your mind. With time, your mind will get the picture and settle into a quiet space.

Do what you can when you can.

Feel free to say no to invitations. At the last minute, if you feel that it is too much for you, you can always change your mind and not go or go late and leave early.

Trust that others are wrapped up in their own lives; they will be happy to see you but also will quickly compensate for your absence, tardiness, or quick exit. Do not regret whatever you decide to do. If it worked out well, wonderful! If you wish you had decided differently, simply chalk this one up and forget about it.

Do what gives you pleasure even if it is only one thing.

A woman tells about the one dependable thing she did in her grief:

> After my husband died, I continued with my household responsibilities and babysitting for my grandchildren as needed. The only other activity I did was crossword puzzles. They were my crutch. For an entire year, that was the activity I depended on.

Every morning, I waited for the newspaper to be delivered with a new crossword puzzle. When I worked the puzzle, I couldn't think about anything else. I couldn't worry about anything. It was the one time in the day when I felt I could focus.

Then, one day, I read in a local newsletter about a volunteer opportunity at a Walking Club in the community. They needed a nurse to take blood pressures. I don't know why, but somehow, I felt ready. As a retired nurse, I began a new life of volunteering. Since then, I have made new friends and am back in the community again. And you know what? I don't even like crossword puzzles anymore.

—Marlene Jordan

Get exercise.

Physical exercise is a mood elevator. It releases feel-good chemicals in your brain, boosts your immune system, and raises your body temperature, all of which may have a calming effect (Mayo Clinic, 2017). Choose activities that give you pleasure. You can exercise alone, in a class, or with friends. Take it easy, though. You have enough on your plate, and an exercise-related injury is not what you need.

Practice gratitude.

At the end of each day, write down things that happened or things you noticed for which you are grateful.

Say a simple thank-you to the sadness that you feel. When you do this, you gain an appreciation for what you are experiencing and a humble and maybe beautiful perspective. You and millions of others are or have experienced sadness. You are not so alone. Your sadness is an important part of human love.

When my sister was diagnosed with stage 4 lung cancer and didn't have a lot of time to live, she practiced gratitude to her lung. Here is part of the email I received from her. It is related to grief and to losing that which is precious.

Although my right lung has certainly been, and continues to be, corrupted by cancer, it deserves a note of thanks. First of all, it has hung in with me for so long and has done a pretty good job of permitting me to breathe and other natural functions. Second of all, for the reason that now that it is harmed and corrupted, it probably needs my thanks and attention even more! That goes for my adrenal gland and my bone, too, where the cancer has spread. So, I think there is a little lesson here—that, if there's a part of your dear body that is bothering you, say thanks anyway, and give it some hefty gratitude for being a part of dear you and trying to survive. I think it will make things a bit better and focus your energies gently and without hard feelings. Well, this is not a grandiose thought, but that's what I am thinking, anyway. Let me know if it works.

Anon and with love,
Sprigs

A woman writes about her experience of gratitude:

My life-partner Mark died suddenly and unexpectedly. I was in a state of shock. Several months after he died, I had the opportunity to spend some time with my brother at his place out of town. I stayed with him for over a week, had a good visit, and participated in the family's daily schedule. Before each meal—breakfast, lunch, and dinner—my brother said a simple grace. I admit that at first, I was a little surprised by this. Yet, at each meal, as I tuned in to this prayer, I felt gratitude and appreciation for the food I was eating and the company of my family. When I would experience gratitude, somehow my grief was lifted for a time. I noticed more of life and felt grateful for the cereal at breakfast, the sandwich at lunch, and the hot meal at night. I have now enlarged this practice of gratitude to include other parts of my life, and I find that it is helping me.

—Genie Sachs

Here are signs to guide you toward getting help.

> **When to get help**
>
> For extended periods, you cannot get out of bed to start your day.
>
> You get no relief from your sadness—all your efforts and those of your loved ones to help you do not work.
>
> You have a sense of doom all the time.
>
> Your intense longing for your loved one increases with time.
>
> You feel as much, if not more, pain as time progresses. The event remains new even years later.
>
> You have suicidal thoughts that will not go away.
>
> You have a plan as to how you will commit suicide.
>
> On a regular basis, you use alcohol and recreational drugs to help you feel better.

Chapter Summary

Sadness is part of being human. Even in the most joyful of times, it is there under the surface. In those times of joy, we call it nostalgia, and we cherish and reminisce about the good times. It is love. We think about our sadness. We feel it. We treasure it. We express it.

The sadness in grief is different. The loss is permanent so there is no going back, no more chances to express your love or get it right. It may take a while to identify sadness because there is so much else and so many other emotions going on at the same time.

There are important distinctions and similarities between the sadness in grief and clinical depression. The sadness in grief is related to your loss. In clinical depression, the sadness is global and chronic. Sometimes the sadness that one experiences in grief can be a clinical depression. If sadness is unrelenting with no relief, and you have an overriding sense of doom all the time, it is time to get help.

Eventually sadness subsides, but it will continue to appear at expected and unexpected times. It resides in all of us and is one of the manifestations of being a person.

Chapter 8

Task 2: To Experience the Pain of Grief—Experiencing Spiritual Pain

> *"Survival often depends on a specific focus: a relationship, a belief, or a hope balanced on the edge of possibility. Or something more ephemeral: the way the sun passes through the hard, seemingly impenetrable glass of a window and warms the blanket, or how the wind, invisible but for its wake, is so loud one can hear it through the insulated walls of a house."*
> —*Elizabeth Tova Bailey in* **The Sound of a Wild Snail Eating**

When you experience a loss in your life, you may experience spiritual pain. If you are an atheist, a secular humanist, or an agnostic, you may not identify what you are going through as spiritual pain. You may not accept that there is such a thing as spirit. Rather, you could see your experience as existential, a crisis of meaning, or a crisis of your philosophy of life.

In this chapter, I will call it spiritual pain. I will describe it and explore ways to alleviate it. I will also discuss the difference between religion and spirituality and the roles each can play in your grief.

Overview of spiritual pain

We seek our place in life: Who am I? What is the meaning of my life? What is my purpose here? What's it all about? All around us are guideposts to help us find our way and answer these questions. Religions and religious leaders, ancient and modern sacred literature, philosophers, scientists, leaders of countries, authors, teachers, family, friends, colleagues, and complete strangers speak about these questions with comfort and assurance.

Many find guidance in their religion, but even so, you will still be on your own individual spiritual journey.

David R. Williams and Michele J. Sternthal (2007), sociologists, describe the differences between spirituality and religion: "Spirituality refers to an individual's attempt to find meaning in life" (2007, p. 47). Religion, they state, is a community experience or a tradition with beliefs and behaviors related to the sacred or supernatural. Religions teach and bless their members through regularly scheduled services, holidays and holy days, and in times of joy and sorrow.

When you attend a religious service, your experience will be unique, based on your personal history, your current outer circumstances, and your current inner state. Your outer circumstance can be your age, your job, your family status, and all that you have experienced.

And then there is the inner state: A cranky and hungry five-year-old; a recently widowed woman who is attending church without her spouse for the first time; a lonely person who is seeking companionship and peace; an ill older person who is grappling with the imminence of death; a teen whose meaning for now is romance; a successful worker who got a promotion; someone else who just lost her job—all of these people may be at the service, but each one experiences the service in a unique way and derives individual meaning from it. This is one's spirituality within the boundaries of a religious group.

By their nature, religions have boundaries of belief. We believe this, not that. We accept this, not that. These very boundaries can be a source of pain, too. The loss you experience may not be accepted or recognized by your religion, e.g., an abortion or a lesbian, gay, bisexual, transgender, or queer (LGBTQ) loss. You may not receive the support you need from your religion or religious community.

We also receive guidance in our day-to-day encounters with one another. How many of us have had the experience of hearing the words of one person that changed our day and maybe our lives? Sometimes, there are no words. We are simply in someone's presence, witnessing her in action, and that presence changes our day and maybe our lives.

We receive guidance from deep within ourselves when we listen to our own intuition and wisdom. Jean Houston recounts an interaction she and her comedy-writer father Jack Houston witnessed. Houston took a delighted Jean (eight years old at the time) to visit the famous ventriloquist Edgar Bergen and his dummy Charley McCarthy in "their" hotel room. The door was open. They slipped in quietly and witnessed not a rehearsal but an interaction between Bergen and Charley. They were having an animated conversation about the ultimate questions of being alive. Bergen was completely involved and asked questions like, "What does it mean to be truly good?" "What is the meaning of life?" "Where is the soul?"

Finally, Houston, an agnostic, coughed and interrupted the conversation. Bergen was embarrassed and taken aback. When questioned, Bergen acknowledged that it was his own mind speaking through Charley, but he also said, "When I ask him these questions and he answers, I haven't the faintest idea what he is going to say and what he says astounds me with his brilliance. It is so much more than I know" (1988, n.p.).

"It is so much more than I know." On one level, Edgar Bergen was a family member, a performer, colleague, human being. However, deep inside there was so much more than he knew on a conscious everyday level. He trusted that inner intuitive self and went there often for knowledge. You don't have to be a ventriloquist to have these inner conversations.

We receive guidance from nature. Sometimes after a long day, I take a walk. I enjoy the natural environment that I am witnessing: trees, shrubs, flowers, insects. At times, as I pass a tree, I may ask, "What message do you have for me?" Or I may just drink in nature's vibrations of the moment: the sun, clouds, a breeze, the colors.

All these ways of seeking inner answers continue when we experience a loss, because we are in a new territory and are starting over. Sister Joan Chittister, Benedictine nun, author, and social activist, says, "Death launches a person into new orbits. It makes us find our way alone again. It requires us to start over. It grows us in ways we never would have chosen but dearly need to learn" (2003, p. 105).

The answers we relied upon may no longer help and may not even be relevant. The people we relied upon may not be helpful, interested, or even there in the way we wished they would be. Our faith in life, in others, in the natural scheme of things, and in God may be challenged. Time stands still. We are alone even in the midst of others.

Ten days after his young adult son died in a car accident, Reverend William Sloane Coffin gave a sermon. He said, "While the words of the

Bible are true, grief renders them unreal. The reality of grief is the absence of God— 'My God, My God, why hast thou forsaken me?' The reality of grief is the solitude of pain, the feeling that your heart is in pieces, your mind's a blank, that 'there is no joy the world can give like that it takes away'" (Lord Byron, cited by Coffin, 2004, n.p.).

Reverend Coffin went on to say that what helped him was simply those who were with him—broken-hearted companions. Those who gave him answers or scriptural quotes left him cold and angry.

His words get to the heart of the matter. His help came not from advice but from the simple and accepting companionship of others. The sacred literature that had sustained him was now unreal. His God was absent. His heart was broken. He was alone in the solitude of pain.

Longing is an element in spiritual pain. Longing to see your loved one, longing for the past, longing to have meaning in your life, to belong, to know who you are and why you are here, to feel at ease and content, and to feel love. In his poem and subsequent treatise, Saint John of the Cross called this "The Dark Night of the Soul." Spiritual longing is not an absence of the answers. Within your longing is the potential to find the answers.

The process of finding answers is an inner search. In his book, *Man's Search for Meaning*, Viktor Frankl (1984), Holocaust survivor, author, and psychiatrist, described his experiences as a prisoner in concentrations camps during World War II. His wife, parents, and brother died in the camps. He says that finding meaning in life is a human being's most important motivation. One can find meaning through love, through work, and through facing and learning from suffering (here he is referring to unavoidable suffering).

How to alleviate spiritual pain

Be with others.

If you are a member of a religion, you may choose to participate in services. Even if you are not inspired by the service, simply being with other people may be healing.

No two people experience a religious service in the same way. Your spirituality can enhance your religious experience. Your religious community experience can enhance your spiritual experience.

After a service, take up your journal, and write about how it affected you and what memories or experiences it brought up.

If you do not participate in a religion, seek out some kind of community to participate in: a support group, talking with others who have experienced a similar loss, a hiking group, an art class, a tai chi class, an online grief community—some kind of group that will inspire spiritual support and good feelings.

If you have people around you who will primarily do just that—just be around you, without giving advice—you are lucky. Well-meaning, well-wishing friends may offer their advice. Sometimes, you can tell that they are talking to themselves rather than you. They are trying to make themselves feel better.

Advice may even make you feel ashamed of your pain or anger. When words of advice are given, first ask yourself, "Is this helpful to me?" If it is not, simply reject it rather than worry about it. If it is helpful, then take it to heart as you continue your journey.

Be alone.

Take some time each day to be alone and quiet. During this uninterrupted time, you can read a poem, say a prayer that is comforting, take a walk in nature, meditate, listen to music, read inspiring or sacred literature.

The "Psalms" are one example of sacred literature that have been with us for 3,000 years. To this day, they bring comfort and inspire hope. The word *psalm* means *song* or *poem*—a song of the soul, written in a poetic form. The "Psalms" are understood on a feeling level, not an intellectual level. In writing the "Psalms," the psalmists drew on their own personal experience, and identified with the seeker. They are teaching not from an intellectual perspective but are sharing their own journey. Their experience inspires us. You can disagree with a teaching, but you cannot disagree with an experience. "...the psalms are thoroughly human documents, reflecting the difficulties of existence, the struggle to remain faithful to ideals, the overcoming of doubt, the fight for victory of the better self, and the conquest of despair..." (Gelberman & Kobak, 1969, p. 136).

Whatever your belief or life's philosophy, sacred literature has something to offer. It reflects the search for truth.

Write.

Writing without reserve is a way for you to identify the pain that you are experiencing. Writing can be good for your health and well-being.

James Pennebaker, a psychologist, conducted a journaling study with college students. One half of the group was asked to write on four consecutive days thoughts and feelings about their most upsetting traumatic experience, an experience that they had not spoken to anyone about. They could write about the same topic on all four days or choose a different topic for each day. The other half was asked to write about mundane things. The group who wrote about a trauma had fewer visits to the college health center, and their immune systems were more enhanced than the control group (Pennebaker, Kiecolt-Glaser, & Glaser, 1988).[6] Jacqueline Olds, a psychiatrist, writes about the students, "Many writers have observed that…it is impossible to write without writing to somebody, even an imagined somebody. In the minds of these students, there must have been a reader or perhaps a listener" (Olds & Webster, 1996, p. 42). I would add that the students were writing to their deepest selves about themselves. This deepest self is the one you experience when you are in a state of peace and equilibrium.

In the midst of your efforts, appreciate the power of time.

An elderly woman once told me, "Patience and time take care of a lot of things, but particularly time." Your efforts to detect and to find meaning in your life take time. A tai chi instructor was encouraging her class to practice regularly. She said that when you practice tai chi, it might feel like nothing is happening, nothing is changing. The practice is like building up a stack of paper. You put down one piece of paper. Each day, you add another. For a long time, it looks like nothing is happening. The stack is not growing. However, after a period of time, you have a ream. Give yourself time.

Occasionally say to yourself, I belong here.

A woman struggled for quite some time after her husband died, trying to feel better and to work on her grief. Still, she had a persistent inner emptiness. She recounts her struggle:

---

[6] The study was conducted in a time period just before exams, when visits to the health center are normally higher than usual.

After my husband died, I felt I was on the outside of everything. I belonged nowhere. There were no answers. I was alone and isolated, on the outside looking in. Everyone else knew what they were doing. I lived with this feeling for quite some time. One day, I had an inner vision. As usual, everyone was in a circle, and as usual, I was on the outside of that circle. But this time I experienced that there was a much bigger circle surrounding all of us. It came to me that the isolation I was experiencing was a part of life, too. I belonged! Life includes this in and out, and we all have our turns in each place. It reminded me of the Frank Sinatra song about falling out of the race and picking yourself up and getting back in. I was outside one circle, yet I belonged in the bigger circle. I felt compassion for myself, and for all people who have ever experienced any kind of loss.

Be open to unexpected glimmers of hope, unlikely sources of guidance.

When crossing a street, we "stop, look, and listen." Throughout your day(s), stop, look and listen for glimmers of hope, glimmers of meaning. When you get a glimmer, write it down. If despair returns, remember the glimmer.

Elisabeth Tova Bailey, author and active outdoorswoman, was stricken with a chronic neurological disorder at the age of thirty-four, which left her weak and immobile. For a number of years, she would improve, and then relapse. Her life was changed. Ms. Bailey's days were spent on her couch in a horizontal position. Her life was hard, her inner questions were hard, and she was on the lookout for answers. A friend gave her a small woodland snail as a gift. For one year, she spent her horizontal days taking care of the snail and intently observing its behavior in a terrarium. She learned as much as she could about it. She wrote:

> I could never have guessed what would get me through this past year—a woodland snail…. I honestly don't think I would have made it otherwise. Watching another creature go about its life… somehow gave me, the watcher, purpose too. If life mattered to the snail and the snail mattered to me, it meant something in my life mattered, so I kept on…(2010, p. 154).

By its nature, spiritual pain is personal. Your spiritual pain may not be shared or understood by others, adding to your experience of aloneness in the universe. If this aloneness becomes too painful, it is time to get help. See the table below for signs to watch for.

> **When to get help**
>
> Your inner longing brings no answers and no relief.
>
> Your spiritual pain is turning into a chronic bitterness about life.
>
> Nothing brings you joy, not even a snail.
>
> The inner emptiness continues, and you feel there is no reason to live. You have suicidal thoughts that will not go away.
>
> You have a plan as to how you will commit suicide.

Chapter Summary

Whenever we experience a loss, our sense of our place in the universe changes. Do we have a place anymore? We can experience deep longing for answers and for relief. The pain of this change can be deep and long lasting, or it can be subtle and unnerving. All the other painful emotions—anger, fear, sadness, depression, longing, guilt, and shame—can add to the fire of spiritual pain.

There is a difference between spirituality and religion. The spiritual seeker is looking for meaning in her life. The religious seeker enjoys a set of beliefs and the comfort and strength of a community.

Religions also have boundaries of beliefs. This exclusiveness can cause the pain of rejection if your loss is not accepted, respected, or recognized by your religion.

A mixture of being with others who are supportive and having alone time helps alleviate spiritual pain. You might read inspirational words, listen to music, meditate or pray, write experiences and insights in your journal, or spend time in nature. Respect your efforts and be aware of the healing power of time. Remember to stop, look, and listen for glimmers of hope. Most important, when you find an answer, remember it! You are adding pages of inner strength to the story of your life.

Chapter 9

Task 3: To Adjust to a World without the Deceased

"Try to strike that delicate balance between a yesterday that should be remembered and a tomorrow that must be created."
—*Earl A. Grollman in* **Living When a Loved One Has Died**

After your loved one dies, you are in the world without him. It is now a different world. Your task is to adjust to this new world. As with all the other tasks, Task 3 can take a very long time, a very short time, or anything in between. In addition, when you work on one task, it has a ripple effect, and you may be attending to the other tasks, too.

A Description of Task 3

Mark Kurlansky (2017), journalist and author describes baseball in Cuba. In Cuba, professional baseball teams play only for their hometown. There is no trading. Once you start on a team, that's where you stay. (There are away games. In that case, everyone piles into buses and goes to root for the home team). At the top are the Havana baseball teams with thousands of fans. Then, there are all the cities, towns, and villages. At each game, the players know the fans. When Cuban baseball players come to the U.S. so that they can expand their opportunities, the hardest adjustment for them is to play baseball in a stadium where they know no one. They are in a sea of strangers.

As you are adjusting to a world without your loved one, you may feel like a Cuban baseball player, newly arrived in the U.S. You are in a sea of strangers. You are still playing the game of life, but the world has changed. You are a stranger in a strange land. Task 3 is to adjust to a world without your loved one.

Your own unique experience of the world—your "take" on it—is your assumptive world. Parkes describes the assumptive world as "…the only world we know, and it includes everything we know or think we know. It includes our interpretation of the past and our expectations of the future, our plans, and our prejudices. Any or all of these may need to change as a result of changes in the life space" (1971, p. 103).

Look at everyone and everything around you, and if you can attach the word "my" to those people or things, they are part of your assumptive world: my spouse, my child, my sibling, my parents, my street, my grocery store, my neighborhood, my city, my country, my school, my garden, my house, my kitchen, my car, my pet, and so on (Parkes, 1971). With every life change, your assumptive world is challenged or enhanced in subtle or dramatic ways. You adjust and create a new world or a new place for yourself.

The death of someone you love is the biggest change, the biggest loss. There is no returning to the world you shared. The person you loved and the world you shared were intertwined. You had a place in each other's lives. Now that your loved one is gone, you are standing alone. Your actions stand alone. They no longer neatly fit into your world. You begin Task 3: to adjust to a world without your loved one.

Although maybe not recognized as such, this task begins immediately upon the death. Unwillingly but necessarily, the widow takes on the daily chores that were shared or were the responsibility of her spouse. A parent whose young child dies continues household and community activities—activities that a short time ago said, "I am a parent."

The more intimate and involved your relationship is with the deceased, the more adjustments you may find yourself making.

There are two worlds: the world you and your loved one were in, and the world you are in now without your loved one. It will seem that everyone else has already adjusted to the new world. Family and friends will initially be with you—coming to the funeral, offering support, and more. However, it won't be long before they seem to have moved on and are treating you like nothing happened. Meanwhile, on the one hand, you are still in a state of suspension, grieving for your loss and adjusting to a new world without your loved one. On the other hand, you may be soaring on ahead, curious about each new adjustment, feeling relief and freedom while your well-wishers stand back in amazement or judgment. Your experience of this task can also change back and forth, from easy to hard and hard to easy. It depends on the nature of your relationship and its history. Each relationship is unique, and each grief experience is unique.

You may also be stuck in Task 3 and find that you cannot make changes in your world. You may keep all the remembrances of your loved one, including clothes, room arrangements, or artifacts for years and years. I do not see this as problematic unless it affects your functioning in the world. If you find that you are unhappy surrounded by these artifacts or that this is the only time that you are at all happy in life, it may be time to reach out for help. Otherwise, please don't worry about it. The other extreme is the person who gives everything away and then regrets doing so. If you are living with that kind of regret, maybe write about your memories, or display a photo of a special artifact or a scene—your loved one with his fishing rod—or draw a picture of an artifact or a scene that is memorable.

Take your time with Task 3. Be gentle with yourself.

Beginning to adjust

You are not a stranger to this process. There are many times during your life when you have to adjust to and make your way in a new world: the first day of school, going away to college, getting a new job, marrying, moving to a new neighborhood, retiring and living in a new world with no colleagues and no 9-to-5 schedule, becoming ill or disabled at any age and living in a slower world with people surging on ahead of you, emigrating to a new country to start anew. The world you knew and were comfortable in no longer works. It may not even be there.

The behaviors that hindered your adjustment to other life changes may appear again during grief. On the other hand, the skills and behaviors that helped your adjustment to other life changes may be useful during grief. What did you do that helped you adjust? What hindered you?

You may have

- reached out to others who were in the same boat;
- hung on to the past for a long time;
- withdrawn from others to get your bearings;

- lost your self-confidence;
- engaged in risky behaviors such as substance abuse;
- asked for help from others who were further along the way than you;
- learned as much as you could about how to adjust to your changed status;
- taken breaks from your new situation;
- made lots of mistakes as you adjusted to the new you;
- took steps forward and took steps back;
- experienced a multitude of various thoughts and feelings—negative and positive;
- missed the past a little or a lot;
- felt a sense of freedom in your new world; and
- felt relief that you were in a new "place."

You may do many of the same things as you adjust to the loss of your loved one. Be on the lookout for things that have hindered your adjustment in the past. These may pop up again.

Each day will bring new adjustments. For a time, each hour will bring new adjustments. There is a wide spectrum of adjustments, depending upon your relationship with the deceased: living with the silence that confirms your loss and engaging in activities without your loved one. Task 3 is a practical task in which you can do something to help yourself adjust. Talk to your loved one. She may be deceased but will continue to be a part of your world. If you ate together, sit in your loved one's place so you don't have to look at an empty chair. Same with sleeping. Sleep in her place or even in a different room for a while. Same with TV. Sit in her chair. Wear his sweater. Reach out to others for your normally shared recreational activities.

Also, do things that do not remind you of your loved one, things that only you enjoy. Search for things to do that only you enjoy. Mix it up, too: doing things that remind you of your loved one and doing things that do not remind you of your loved one.

Give yourself compliments and appreciation for your efforts. This is a good time to join a support group, where you can exchange ideas and share how you are thinking and feeling, how you are doing, what skills you are learning, and your successes and failures.

In facilitating bereavement support groups for widowed spouses, I learned to witness non-grief discussions that were important in working on Task 3—sharing ideas and experiences about traveling alone, cooking for one, and entertaining guests. There were meetings with lots of grief going on and meetings devoted primarily to new skills and new practical adjustments.

Beyond the beginning adjustment period, when the adjustment can keenly be felt, are life's anniversary days. An anniversary is a recurring event, commemorating and/or celebrating a notable day. Anniversaries bring back memories, which may set you back into your grieving and make you sad. Or they may show you how far you have come and give you a new appreciation for yourself. They may bring up feelings of happiness and gratitude. You may experience the presence of your loved one. As you adjust to a world without your loved one, anniversary days are important because they will reveal to you where you are.

There are three kinds of anniversaries of importance in grief: traditional anniversaries, anniversaries of the heart, and painful anniversaries. But really, every day is an anniversary of sorts, with its morning, noon, and night; its sun, clouds, and rain; its noise and silence; its people who are a part of that day and its people who are absent; its schedule of events such as meal times, nap times, times of leaving and times of returning. The mini-anniversaries are important, yet it is the big ones that can give you perspective and vision as to where you are, where you may need to go, and how far you have come. These recurring events bring into stark relief the absence of your loved one and the changes in your assumptive world.

Traditional anniversaries—the grand performance anniversaries—are the holidays, such as Christmas, Hanukkah, July 4, Memorial Day; and family/friend events such as birthdays, graduations, and wedding anniversaries. The community and/or your family prepare and celebrate. The expectation, and even pressure, is on everyone to join in, and, at least, to acknowledge the event.

The anniversaries of the heart are more private and perhaps remembered only by you as significant. I attended a wedding where people gave a blessing or advice to the bride and groom. One woman stood up and said that her marriage had its own special rituals and activities that were created over time and that all marriages have these unique events. She wished the couple well, and her hope for them was that they would enjoy creating these special repetitious moments. These are anniversaries of the heart that only you know about—little moments that were embedded in your relationship. In marital, friend, parental, and even collegial relationships, there are special rituals that are unique.

Anytime you experience a grief reminder that triggers a grief reaction, it may be an anniversary of the heart. For example, you walk by a local coffee shop and smell the coffee. Suddenly, you are transported back to special cups of coffee with your loved one. You see children playing and remember visits to the playground with your child. You go to a sports bar, and you remember those sports conversations with your buddy. What are the anniversaries of your heart?

Painful anniversaries are the events related solely to your loss: the date of diagnosis, the date of death, the day of the week of the death, the time of the death, the month of the death, the place of the death. Anniversaries bring back memories and the realization of your loss.

Adjustments for traditional anniversaries.

Many of the things that help you to honor traditional anniversaries are also applicable to anniversaries of the heart and painful anniversaries.

Plan.

When you know that a special date is coming up, plan to honor or celebrate it in a way that is comfortable for you. Waiting until the day comes may leave you lonely and depressed.

Be wary of the word *should*.

Should implies an obligation. "I should cook Thanksgiving dinner." "I should go to that party." "I should have the whole family over for dinner." Try to do things only if you want to do them. If you should cook the holiday turkey, try putting the word *want* in there. "I want to cook the holiday turkey." If you don't want to, then don't. Or leave the door open. Instead of *should*, say *might*. "I might cook the holiday turkey." This leaves room for some creativity and innovation (Smith, 2006). Maybe you'll order a cooked turkey.

Talk about your wishes.

Talk with your family and/or friends about how you would like to celebrate the holiday. People may come forward to ask you how they can help. Remember not many of us know how to help grieving people. Giving people something to do helps us all learn how to help.

Loved ones may not understand how you may feel about a holiday, and you may have to tell them. Do you want to celebrate the holiday as you always did? Would you like to simplify it? Would you like to skip it entirely? Would you like to celebrate the holiday somewhere else? At someone else's house? On a cruise? At a restaurant? Would you like to celebrate in a different way?

Change your plans.

Leave room in your planning so that you are not trapped. You may have always been the host for the celebration. The day arrives, and there is no escape for you. Delegate someone else to oversee the celebration or to be your partner. Then, when the day comes, and you realize that being alone or just showing up for part of the time would be the most helpful to you, you can do this.

Create a new way of celebrating.

Instead of honoring your loved one's birthday at home, you could celebrate with others at a restaurant. For a major holiday, you could offer volunteer services in a community setting or a place of worship.

Occasionally avoid the holiday.

Holidays and anniversaries are intense reminders. It may be helpful for you to be with others on these days. However, you may choose to occasionally skip a holiday entirely by going on a trip with your family or friends or being alone if you feel comfortable with that.

Watch your stress level.

You may have high expectations of yourself for your participation in these events. However, holiday stress and the presence of grief can make the celebration difficult. Pull back and think about it. What is it that you feel comfortable doing? Listen to your own intuition, and do what feels best for you—everything? nothing? something? As you choose the events that you would like to attend, be mindful of the people there. Will they help you to be happy, or will they increase your stress?

Reach out to others.

The others can be family and friends, and people who have experienced a similar loss and with whom you can derive mutual support. The others can just be people you meet in a casual way such as a clerk in a store, a bus driver. Say a friendly "hello." Receive their love, too. As you are adjusting to a world without your loved one, you are becoming comfortable in this new world. Some days, these things will work, and your reaching out will be rewarding. At other times, not so much or not at all. Don't give up. If you are an older person who may already have experienced many losses, loneliness can become a constant undercurrent. By reaching out, you are making connections.

There are support groups where you can give and receive encouragement. Searching for the right group is like shopping for a car—you may have to test drive a few to find the one that is a good fit for you. If a group is not a good fit, don't be discouraged. There are others out there. A good rule of thumb for deciding whether a group is the right one for you: attend the group more than once before you decide to leave.

Family may not be supportive. Remember, they, too, may be grieving and may be unable to help. Widowed people are sometimes critical of their adult children who don't understand. Their children are also grieving, albeit in a different way, and for a parent rather than a spouse. Their world has also changed.

If your family was not supportive before your loved one's death, their unsupportive behavior could continue. You may at times have to lower your expectations of others during your grief, as painful as that is. On the other hand, your unsupportive family may surprise you.

Make up a ritual.

Place a photo of your loved one in a visible place. Many people choose cemetery visitations and religious services on special holidays. You might go to a favorite place in nature or write a letter or speak aloud to your loved one about how you are doing. Writing and speaking are activities that slow down the mind and help you to focus.

Suspend judgment of yourself.

Sometimes, you will say yes to a holiday/anniversary event invitation and regret it. Sometimes, you will say no and regret it. Be kind to yourself, and accept that you will not always decide "correctly." The anticipation of the event may be harder than the event. These events may look like huge approaching thunderstorms, with dark clouds and wind. When they are over, the initial reaction is the same as the aftermath of a real thunderstorm: quiet, time to survey the damage, and gratitude that it is over and that you made it through.

Remember the essence and the meaning of the holiday.

The challenge of holidays is that there are so many memories of past holidays. To get some perspective and relief, try to focus on the universal meaning of the event.

Whether or not you celebrate Christmas, it is a holiday that is visible from October through early January. What is the underlying universal meaning of Christmas for you? Humility? The search for the truth? Generosity? Authenticity? Love? A new beginning? Faith? Hope?

What does a birthday mean to you? That each person has a place on this earth? We each have something to contribute? We belong here? We are important, whether we are a king or a pauper? We review the past and say hello to the future?

I used question marks because the meaning is different for each person.

Remember surrender.

Your self-effort may sometimes strengthen grieving thoughts and feelings, add energy to your pain, and make your adjustment seem hard if not impossible. When this happens, remember the word surrender. Surrender to the feelings and thoughts that come up. Just let them occur without remedy or plans. Sometimes, this surrender will help. You may define surrender in a military way: I lose and surrender. Instead, view this kind of surrender as if you are riding the waves of the ocean, or diving into the waves before they crest, rather than standing up to the waves and being knocked over. When you choose to surrender to grief's thoughts and feelings for a time, you are riding the waves of grief, you are diving into them, and you are flowing with them.

Adjustments for anniversaries of the heart – anniversaries known only to you and the deceased.

Reminisce with others.

Say the name of your loved one. Don't wait for others to bring up your loved one and your loss. They might be afraid to. Ask others to share with you their own memories of your loved one, and to listen to your memories.

Avoid and connect.

If there is a special place that you frequented, it may be helpful to avoid it for a while. The opposite is just as true. Going to that special place may help you to feel connected with your loved one. Follow your intuition.

Make up a new anniversary of the heart.

Go to your special place with friends and family or go to a new place. Celebrate your loved one's birthday and place a photo of her at her place. Set a place for her at the table for family celebrations. Cook his favorite meal and share it with friends and family. Celebrate these new anniversaries of the heart with memories and stories.

Adjustments for painful anniversaries – events that remind you of circumstances surrounding your loss.

Create a shared ritual.

If you create a ritual with another person, what that person can say is limited and somewhat proscribed. He may not be as likely to change the subject. He may feel more comfortable because there is something he can do to help. The following examples of shared rituals can help to connect you to others and to the deceased:

- visiting the grave site;
- going through photographs together;
- reading poetry together;
- praying together;
- going to favorite places of the deceased;
- sharing a moment of silence; and/or
- lighting a candle.

Create an alone ritual.

An alone ritual can be the same as a shared ritual. Instead of sharing a ritual with someone else, you create a ritual and participate in it alone. Alone rituals help you to go inside and feel an inner connection to your loved one. When you complete the ritual, no matter how short it is, you will hopefully experience some inner peace—and power, too.

Participate in traditional and cultural rituals.

Make "in memory of" donations to organizations such as a hospital or hospice. Attend memorial events.

Avoid and connect.

You can choose alternative routes in your car to avoid passing the hospital or the intersection where your loved one died. Or you can choose the same route as a special connection to your loved one.

As stated before, there is no timeline for the tasks. Task 3 can take a short time or a long time. You are the judge as to how you are doing in your work on this task. Here are some signs that might help you decide to reach out for help.

> **When to Get Help**
>
> You cannot give away, change, or get rid of any remembrances of your loved one, and it has been several years since the death. Rather than giving you pleasure, these objects seem to increase your grief, or only give you temporary comfort.
>
> You are feeling discouraged and depressed about your present life and yearn incessantly for the past. There is no joy in your life, or relief from your grief.
>
> You find that you are angry most of the time because people do not understand and keep pressuring you to move on in your life. It is normal to feel angry about this, but if the loss has occurred several years ago, then it may be time to get help.

Chapter Summary

Task 3 is adjusting to a world without your loved one. The world that you and your loved one shared was part of your assumptive world, the world that you were used to waking up to in the morning and leaving at the end of the day as you went to sleep. This world is unique to you. Anything to which you can add the word "my" is part of this world. When your loved one died, your assumptive world changed.

During your life your assumptive world has probably changed many times—going to school, starting a new job, marrying, moving, having children, etc. You have adjusted to these changes in ways that were helpful to you and in ways that may have hindered your progress too.

When your loved one dies, changes in your assumptive world can be daunting. In the beginning, each day, each hour may bring new adjustments as you carry out your activities of daily life alone. You learn to make practical adjustments and you learn new skills so that you will become more at ease in your new world. These adjustments can take a long time or a short time, depending on your relationship with your loved one. If you were very close, there may be more adjustments to make. If you were a caregiver for a long time, perhaps you already made many adjustments before your loved one died.

Beyond the beginning adjustments, the days that can be the hardest are the anniversary days. There are three kinds of anniversaries:

- *traditional anniversaries* that are shared by your community and/or family;
- *anniversaries of the heart* that are more private and perhaps only known to you and your loved one; and
- *painful anniversaries* that are related to the circumstances of the death.

Your choices are to honor these anniversaries, to modify them, and sometimes to completely avoid them. Be gentle with yourself and do what feels the best to you. Trust that with each anniversary, you are making your way through grief.

As you adjust to a world without your loved one you are incorporating your loss into your life, you are creating a new world. What would this new world look like to you?

- one where you would feel safe
- one where you would feel needed
- one where you would belong
- one where your life would have meaning
- one where you would have hope for the future

And yes, your loved one is a part of this new world (see Chapter 10).

Grief is a normal process in which we as humans adjust to a loss and move on in our lives. The adjustment period is important. As you make it through each day, at times you may not feel safe, needed, like you belong, that your life has meaning, or that there is hope for the future. You may also have moments of joy and laughter, you may make new discoveries, and glimmers of hope may appear. Talk with supportive people and with your deceased loved one about what you are experiencing. This is all part of adjusting to a world without your loved one.

Julie Potter, MSW, LCSW

Chapter 10

Task 4: To Embark on a New Life While Establishing a Place in Your Heart for Your Deceased Loved One

"You have to love them in their presence and in their absence."
—*Harold Ivan Smith in* Red Letter Days

Task 4 involves embarking on a new life while establishing a place in your heart for your deceased loved one. Another way of saying this is to find an enduring connection with the deceased in the midst of embarking on a new life (Worden, 2009). This is a twofold task: moving forward and remembering. They go hand in hand. The past informs the present. We move forward into the future and honor the past.

Moving forward and remembering

Freud believed we had to sever the bonds with those who died in order to move on with our life, and on to new relationships. We had to say good-bye. In modern language, we had to experience "closure." The energy that we put forth in our relationship with the deceased now had to be directed toward new relationships.

Before Freud's ideas gained in popularity, the common wisdom was that grief continued throughout life as intermittent sadness and brokenheartedness; frequent reminders; prayers to, and one-sided conversations with, the deceased about life events (mistakes, successes, losses and growth); and continuing and deepening appreciation for the person who died. The past informed the present, gave teachings to the present, gave blessings to the present, and gave purpose to the future. This is a more realistic and kinder view of grief. When you grieve in this way you are not crazy, you are not so alone, you are connected to your loved one, and you are connected to all those who have come before you. Many cultures refer to this as ancestor worship in which the lives of those who die have continual meaning in the present life of individuals and the community. Grieving people are not left entirely to their own devices. The dead are not forgotten. Life and death are interdependent.

You don't have to be old to be an ancestor. You can be a child. Whatever your age, your life has meaning and knowledge to impart and you help the grieving person. Your teachings are not always positive. A relationship that was full of conflict and fear has different information for the griever than a relationship of love and trust.

We are now appreciating the wisdom of ancestor worship, the idea that the relationship does not end. "While the intensity of the relationship with the deceased may diminish with time, the relationship does not disappear. We are not talking about living in the past, but rather recognizing how bonds formed in the past can inform our present and our future" (Silverman & Klass, 1996, p. 17).

John R. Jordan (2016), clinical psychologist and grief specialist says, "Your task is not to let go. Your task is to find a different way to hold on" (n.p.). It is natural to have a continuing bond with those who have gone before us, to experience signs of their presence, to dream about them, to think about them fondly and with new insights, to be inspired by the lives they lived, to seek their forgiveness, to forgive them, to learn from their example, and to reminisce about them. This new way of holding on helps us in the present and gives us hope.

You discover over and over, maybe for the rest of your life, the meaning of your relationship with the person who died. Whether you were very close or not, whether your relationship was short or long, whether the death was expected or not, the meaning of the relationship changes over time as you yourself change over time. You no longer have the person on this physical plane to discuss this. However, on a mental or spiritual level, you see the qualities of the deceased, and you recognize the challenges he faced from the vantage point of years. More and more you may appreciate who he was and who you are.

Movement is the hallmark of life. To experience gratitude for the movement, to appreciate the creative movement of your life, gives power to Task 4.

The following story describes how a woman working on Task 4 appreciated a new experience while also remembering her spouse:

> When I went to visit my husband's columbarium at Arlington National Cemetery, I met another widow who was visiting her husband's gravesite. We struck up a conversation, and I was overjoyed to be with someone who shared my grief and experience. We left the cemetery together and spent a leisurely afternoon talking. And yes, laughing! All in all, it was a beautiful day. Here I was at my husband's final resting place, and I'd made a new friend.
>
> My meeting a new friend a year after Dave's death made me realize that I was adjusting to this terrible change. I could make a new start.
>
> During the nine months before we had hospice at home, my severe anxiety was relieved by daily visits from our devoted daughter. I cared for Dave morning, noon and night. Chemotherapy took its toll. When I left for an errand, I was acutely aware of his state of mind without me. This was unlike both of us who had been so devoted to each other, yet independent. His illness bound us together in close proximity.
>
> I now live in a high-rise. When I go out on my balcony and see Arlington Cemetery in the distance, it gives me a warm feeling to know that I'll be joining Dave again. How blessed I was to have him.
>
> —Rosemary Bowen

Julie Potter, MSW, LCSW

How to move forward and remember

Be open to new experences and appreciate your efforts. If you make mistakes, that means you are human being. Just keep beginning again. The following are things that you can do to help with Task 4.

Practice gratitude.

If you do a million things, and think, hey, I'm on the right track, those things can be stale and even shallow if you are not grateful. Gratitude enlivens experiences.

Whether it has been one day, one month, one year, one decade, say an inner thank-you. This may not always be easy.

Gratitude opens the heart and helps you to be open to new experiences. As you say thank you and appreciate the people and things that are around you, you may move through life with more grace and less striving.

Gratitude reinforces the place your loved one has in your life, as someone who has come before, as an ancestor. Even if the deceased is a young person, she still is an ancestor. Even if the deceased is your enemy, he is still an ancestor. With gratitude, you are honoring the memory of the person who died as you move forward in your life.

Try new things, savor the same old things.

Be open to new experiences. Consider doing volunteer work. Learn about something you are interested in, in the library or on the Internet. Then, check locally for resources on that topic. Learn a new skill.

Check in with friends. I worked with a bereavement volunteer who did this regularly. He would call his friends just to say "hi" and catch up. Maintaining contact with others is a great way to inspire new experiences.

If you are working as an employee or as a volunteer, your job can become your anchor. At first, this may not be easy, but it may give you comfort and renewed purpose as time goes on.

What are some of the same old things, the tried-and-true things, that you like to experience? Gardening, socializing with people, taking walks, hobbies? Savor the old.

Talk to your loved one. Talk about your loved one.

Say whatever you want to your loved one. It can be a prayer: please help me with this situation. If you were here, what would you do? It can be a rush of emotion and exasperation: Why did you have to leave? If only things had been different! It can be a simple and gentle exposition of your day and your experiences. Cemetery visitations are an opportunity to talk to your loved one.

When talking with others, share memories and encourage others to share their memories. Start with "Remember when?" sentences. Sharing of memories helps to link the past with the present.

Be open to experiences of the deceased.

Whether you believe serendipitous experiences are real or that they are coincidental or simply your imagination, be open to them. Many people feel comforted by the feeling of the presence of their loved one, and little happenings that can only be a sign of the deceased. These experiences help you on your way.

Use turning points as remembering points.

Turning points are events that mark a change: a birthday, a graduation, a wedding, a funeral, a new baby, a family reunion, a new house, a new neighborhood, an illness, a breakup of a relationship, a new job, or a lost job. How would your loved one experience, enjoy, or deal with this turning point? Turning points are special opportunities to connect with the memory of your loved one.

Throughout this book, I have talked about the power of rituals and how they can show you where you are. Turning points can be a natural time for a ritual.

Celebrate your loved one's birthday with his favorite meal and favorite cake. People may want to talk about those who have died but they do not necessarily have those desires at the same time. We may share a memory, and it may seem to disappear into the ethers. Yet, if a special day is chosen, everyone can share, everyone can listen and appreciate, and the energy is unified.

Celebrate your birthday with your favorite meal and cake. Celebrate your own learning and accomplishments. How have you changed? How have you grown? What things are you proud of doing?

For an individual ritual, you can write a letter to your loved one, or journal about what you are thinking and feeling.

Connect to your center.

The renowned philosopher, Joseph Campbell (1987), said of his everyday life that it was busy with people, obligations, and events pulling at him continually. Every day he reserved one hour just for himself to regain his inner power and equanimity, to do only what he wanted to do. What would your one hour look like?

Each task is challenging, and Task 4 is no exception. Here are some signs that might help you decide to reach out for help.

> **When to get help**
>
> The first four things listed below can be a normal part of grief. Take note of them, if these ideas persist for a very long time, or for an amount of time that is uncomfortable for you.
>
> Moving into the future seems impossible.
>
> You feel discouraged and depressed most of the time about your present life.
>
> You yearn for the past, and it gives you deep pain to know that you cannot go there.
>
> There is no way that you could love anyone else.
>
> Escaping into substance abuse is your way of coping.

Chapter Summary

Task 4 is embarking on a new life while establishing a place in your heart for your deceased loved one.

When your loved one dies, your loved one is gone. However, playwright Robert Anderson says, "Death ends a life, but it does not end a relationship" (1970, n.p.). The relationship continues through memories, serendipitous events, dreams, reminders, celebrations, and rituals. The bond with your loved one continues as you embark on a new life.

Freud's idea about grief was that in order to move on to the future, you had to close the door to the past. Yet now we know that keeping the door to the past open can help us move into the present and into the future. In other cultures, this is called ancestor worship. Those who die continue to have a place in the lives of those who are left behind. Prayers are offered for the ancestors and to the ancestors. They are asked for protection and guidance. This gives families and friends, and at times the whole community, comfort, hope, and a pathway to the future.

As the grieving person, you can find the meaning of your life becoming clearer as you frequently appreciate and remember the panorama of your loved one's life. Your loved one is a participant in your journey, albeit on a subtle level. As you try a mixture of trying new things and enjoying old things, you slowly gain a changed identity and comfort in your new world. You create a new world—a new assumptive world—and your loved one is a part of that world. The discovery of meaning is a lifelong unfolding. Grief is a lifelong unfolding.

Julie Potter, MSW, LCSW

Part 3
SPECIAL CONSIDERATIONS

Part 3 includes a discussion of sudden death, ambiguous loss, and the different styles of grieving.

Julie Potter, MSW, LCSW

Chapter 11

Sudden Death

> *"When you're in the middle of a story, it isn't a story at all but rather a confusion, a dark roaring, a blindness, a wreckage of shattered glass and splintered wood, like a house in a whirlwind or else a boat crushed by the icebergs or swept over the rapids, and all aboard are powerless to stop it. It's only afterwards that it becomes anything like a story at all, when you're telling it to yourself or someone else."*
> —*Actor, Michael Polley*[7]

In this chapter, I will discuss the phenomenon of sudden death, the different kinds of sudden death, and suggestions to help you in your grieving.

Overview of sudden death

Sudden death will continue to happen to human beings. Religious traditions address this issue. Jesus reminded his followers to be prepared to die because we know neither the day nor the hour. Other traditions say, "Live as if this is your last day on this earth, and at the same time, live as if you have a thousand years to live." In other words, plan your life as if you have all the time in the world, but be ready to die right now.

All species, in order to survive, strive to avoid danger. They are not always successful. The hawk whisks the mouse from the field. The bear scoops up the salmon. The hunter kills the deer who is dining. A woman innocently opens the door of her home to a murderer. A bug inhales some

---
7 As related by Sarah Polley (2012).

bug spray. A shooter sprays bullets into a crowd. Our own body may suddenly and with little warning, experience a heart attack.

The threat of danger is an undercurrent in all animals. Parkes and Prigerson (2010) put it this way:

> Human beings bring to this age-old situation, not a terrifying and dangerous set of teeth and claws, but a highly efficient memory and decision-making mechanism capable of guiding their approach to any problematic situation. It is this success in 'attacking' problems in advance that has given us a distinct advantage over other species. It also leaves us with the need to anticipate events that may never happen and to prepare ourselves in retrospect for disasters that are already past. In other words, we are the only animal who worries and agonizes (p. 44).

Day in and day out, we give little reminders to our loved ones and to ourselves to protect us from danger and from death. We all hope these reminders will protect us, and we dread the day that they don't.

- "Make sure you lock the door."
- "Text me when you get home."
- "Be careful."
- "If I'm not home, don't answer the door."
- "Don't talk with strangers."
- "Please follow your doctor's advice."
- "You are driving too fast."
- "Watch your step."
- "Look both ways when crossing the street."

For a loved one to suddenly die without warning is a fearful thing to consider. For us to die suddenly is a fearful thing to consider, too. Could this be why people sometimes say, "I'd like to die in my sleep"? We would sidestep our fears of death because we would not be awake when it happened. As Woody Allen (1975, p. 99) said, "I'm not afraid to die; I just don't want to be there when it happens."

Harnessing the Power of Grief

When a sudden death occurs, your reactions as the survivor are magnified and more acute than if the death is expected. You did everything right, yet he died. There is no time to say goodbye. Your world unexpectedly changes in an instant. The meaning of your life has suddenly changed. You may feel that no meaning remains. Edward K. Rynearson, a psychiatrist, tells us: in a sudden death, there is "no time or space for caregiving or relinquishing" (2010, p. 180). No time for preparation or control. No second chance for the survivor to get it right just one more time.

When a death is expected, whether you are the dying person, the caregiver, or the "survived by" person, you can participate in the dying process and its decisions. You have some control: what medical treatments to accept or reject, who to see, who to forgive, who to ask forgiveness of, what celebratory events to attend, what special places to go to, what legacy to leave behind, what estate to leave behind, what the funeral will be like, etc. After death, the memories may be difficult to bear for the "survived by" person, but they can also eventually bring comfort. You might not have done everything you could, but you did the best you could.

Even in an expected death, there may be elements of the dying process that leave you as the survivor traumatized and maybe also betrayed: how your loved one looked while getting treatment for a disease process or wound care; the final exit of the body to the funeral home; your own reaction to the dying process and the death that are "out of character" for you; personality changes of the dying person that are directed towards you, such as angry outbursts, rejection, even hatred. Following the death, your grief may be unimportant or immaterial to other people. Some people may even tell you that your grief experience is small compared to the suffering of others, that it is time for you to move on. You cannot judge or compare suffering. Like a small container that is full of gas, or a large container that is full of gas, they both are full (Frankl, 1984).

When my sister died after a long illness, several of us were present. The hospice nurse came to the house. We helped to prepare her body and chose clothes for her final outfit. We were sad, but there was also some relief, and laughter, too. We all felt very close to one another. About two hours later, the funeral hearse arrived. Two attendants came into the house to remove the body. As they took my sister's body out of the house and we saw her body being lifted into the hearse, suddenly we were all silent. I felt alone and stunned. That was the hardest part of her death. At that point, I was inconsolable. Nothing helped. To this day, that memory brings me deep sorrow.

People who have been living with an incurable and life-threatening illness for a long time may openly talk about their mortality. The end may be in sight, but there is still one more thing to do, one more treatment, one more day, and one more family event to live for. Life goes on, hope goes on, even in the face of death. Weisman's "middle knowledge" may come into play many times before your loved one dies—"I know my loved one is gravely ill, and all treatments have stopped, but I still have hope she will get well." Survivors may struggle with the effects of middle knowledge after the death and feel very guilty about it. "Why didn't I see it coming?" "It was so clear. Why didn't my doctor see it?" Not only you and your loved one but also your medical treatment team may have been experiencing middle knowledge.

Sudden losses range from natural causes that affect all ages: miscarriage and stillbirth, Sudden Infant Death Syndrome, sudden medical events for all ages of people; natural disasters; accidents, which, unfortunately primarily affect young people under 40 (this includes children); suicide; homicide; military deaths; and deaths caused by terrorist attacks.

In the following section, I will describe different kinds of sudden death, their characteristics, and what can help. There is a large and growing accumulation of literature focused solely on this topic. Complete discussion of this topic is beyond the scope of this book. This chapter will provide an entry point into the larger body of literature.

Different kinds of sudden death

Natural death

A person may die suddenly of natural causes. Or he may have been ill, and was recovering, when he suddenly dies. The death is a surprise, and there may be frightening memories associated with it, such as the cause of the death, the appearance of the body, or where the death occurred.

An important part of grieving a sudden loss is to first figure out what happened—how and why the death occurred. Since it was sudden, the answers may not be readily apparent. If it was a medical event, you may talk with your doctor, review the medical record, request an autopsy, and talk with others to discover "Did we see this coming?" "Why did this happen?" Even though the death was sudden, the lifestyle may have predicted an expected death, e.g., if someone had many underlying medical problems or may have abused alcohol or drugs.

Natural disasters

Natural disasters can devastate entire neighborhoods and communities. There may be loss of life and the loss of meaningful things in the environment: property (both public and private), jobs, and familiar natural elements such as trees and whole swaths of landscape that have been damaged or destroyed. Survivors look for the remains or mementoes of the people who died.

Accidental death

Most accidental deaths happen at home and, unfortunately, a number of these deaths are of young children from aspiration, drowning, falling, poisoning, or an accidental shooting. The surviving parents and other family members are traumatized. The answers are traumatizing. too. One minute all is well. The next minute your toddler has taken a fatal fall. Car accidents affect all people. However, teenagers, young adults, and older people have higher involvement in car accidents—young people because of inexperience on the road, bravado, peer pressure, driver distraction, or substance abuse; older people because of medical and physical issues such as a slower response time, orthopedic problems, and vision impairment.

Death of a child

Of all human relationships, the parent-child relationship is the most intense—"physically, psychologically, and socially" (Rando, 1991, p. 163). Parents create their child, protect her from harm, and nurture her to adulthood. Many would say that it is the most important human relationship. There is no other relationship in which one is cared for in such a protective, nurturing, and eye-to-the-future way. For a child, the parent is the first idea of God in human form. Your parents have all the answers (at least when you are young). You are cared for, loved, caressed, and protected.

For you as a parent, your child carries your hopes for the future, and your genes into the future. It doesn't matter how old your child is when he or she dies. It is not the natural course of events. Added to your grief is the sense of guilt and even failure that you were not able to prevent the death and protect your child from harm.

Terrorism

I am sad to include terrorism, but it is now an acknowledged fact of modern life, here and all over the world. The Online Merriam Webster Dictionary (2020) defines terror as "violence that is committed by a person, group or government in order to frighten people and to achieve a political goal." In certain countries of the world, whole segments of the population live with the constant threat of terrorism.

In an open society like ours, people freely and innocently participate in life in locations that are generally considered safe—schools, resorts and vacation spots, places of employment, airplanes, subways, and trains. Granted, we need to be wary of travelling especially in high crime areas, but generally, we feel safe. Yet without warning, a terrorist attack can occur.

The perpetrator(s) of violent acts may be someone with severe mental problems or a member of a terrorist group. When an attack occurs, we are all affected. We know it could happen to anyone at anytime and anywhere. In the US, the term shooter is now a common word in our vocabulary. The shooter is a terrorist, terrorizing and traumatizing school children and adults who innocently go about their days.

In 2007, two shooters randomly shot pedestrians in the suburban Washington, DC, area. Many people were killed over a period of several months. I didn't even live near where any of the shootings had occurred, and there was an infinitesimally small chance that I would be shot. Still, in my daily walks, I walked on the side of the street against traffic rather than with traffic so I would hopefully see what was coming rather than be shot from behind. When I stopped at a gas station to pump gas, I was wary and looked furtively in every direction, aware that one of the shooting victims had been shot at a gas pump and that I was a sitting duck.

Suicide

Although attitudes are changing, suicide remains a taboo in our culture. Many Western religions have proscriptions against it. Survivors have to deal with both the trauma and grief of the loss, guilt of their own (could I have prevented this?), guilt that is superimposed by the culture (you should have prevented this), and many feelings directed at the deceased: feelings of rejection and anger toward the deceased. And so many questions that will never be completely answered: How could you do this? Why did you do this? How could you doubt my love? What did I do wrong? Added to the trauma of suicide, survivors may be questioned by the police, and even initially be under investigation for homicide before suicide is confirmed.

As we learn more about the suffering of those with mental illnesses (depression, psychosis, schizophrenia)—the toll of loneliness, the burden of chronic disease, the particular susceptibility of teens to commit suicide, and the dangerous side effects of drugs whether prescribed or not—we are coming to have more compassion for both the victims of suicide and the survivors. Still, Carl Aksel Sveen and Frederik A. Walby, psychologists, who studied survivors of suicide say, "The evidence clearly suggests that suicide survivors experience a significantly higher level of rejection compared with all other bereaved groups, including accident survivors. It seems that suicide survivors commonly experience suicide as an act of intentional rejection" (2008, p. 24). The survivor may feel rejected by his culture and by the person who committed suicide—the "victim."

There is yet another reason for grief. "Though the dying was highly intentional, the murderer and the victim disappeared in the same act. There is no one left to apprehend or punish" (Rynearson, 2001, p. 118).

In general, survivors of suicide are shocked and traumatized. In 1940, artist Mark Rothko wrote to the painter Clyfford Still: "This has been the darkest winter of my life—why and what I hardly know myself.... Ironically enough of my pictures have never been more ecstatic. People will say what a cheerful guy I must be." Rothko committed suicide in 1970 (Sheets, 2016). Rothko's statement captures the state of a depressed person, the disconnect between how a person may feel and how everyone else views him.

For others, their grief may also be paired with relief that a long history of suffering for the individual and the whole family system is ended, albeit in a traumatic way. One of the bereaved I interviewed, an author and counselor, Judith Boivin writes compellingly about her son:

> My son Paul completed suicide when he was twenty-two years old. He hung himself. When he died, I sat with the pain all the

time. For 5-6 years, I kept looking for the answers. Why? Why? Why? Paul had lived with depression and drug abuse problems for years. I had kept trying and hoping that he would get better. He frequently rejected my efforts, and me. When he died, I wondered if I was a bad mother, and what I had done wrong. I was filled with self-doubt, feelings of rejection and guilt, rather than hope.

I will never really know why Paul committed suicide, but I do know a lot more about myself. I've learned that I spent my life securing the parameters – being in control, finding answers, protecting answers. I have learned that the answer is less important now. Rather it is the process of the search, and everything met on the way. I've learned that my need to be in control was an illusion. I couldn't control Paul. I couldn't control his actions. Although he came through me, he is separate from me. Yet I will always be his mother. When people ask me how many children I have, I say five, four who are living and one who died. The more I understand myself the more I can contribute to others in a more meaningful way.

Paul's suicide and our subsequent grief catapulted all of my family into our own different paths of healing and inner discovery. His suicide brought us closer. He continues to be a presence, an awareness in our lives. Yes, the pain is still here too, but it's different now. The guilt and the shame are gone. Instead the pain is a poignant recognition that I no longer have the privilege of his being with me. Even now, sometimes we will say, "Could there be a 'why'?" But then we let the question go. The answer is no longer important. Rather it is our journey toward it that matters. It's like we are making space for it all to be ok. If it is not ok, we do not have the freedom to continue our lives in a productive and a happy way.

For me, a group called Survivors of Suicide (a local group under the American Foundation for Suicide Prevention AFSP) was a first step toward healing. I continue to be active with this group.

—Judith Boivin

Homicide

The crime of murder against a loved one is also a crime against the state. In a matter of speaking, the state is also the victim. The criminal must be discovered, apprehended, and tried in a court of law in order to both serve justice and protect the community. There is the underlying possibility that the murderer will not be found. The homicide becomes public, with news and media coverage, police investigations, and a trial and sentencing.

Survivors are in an environment that gives them little support and that may add to the trauma, with public repetition of the traumatic details of the death in both the criminal justice system and in the media. The focus is the victim of the homicide and the murderer, not the surviving family members, friends, neighbors, and colleagues. Survivors may also be considered suspects, which may significantly add to their trauma. Their grief may not even begin in earnest until legal proceedings are completed.

Military trauma

In war, death is a constant threat amid unending scenes of tragedy and destruction. Fellow soldiers may die in battle, and there may be little time to grieve because one needs to be ready for the next attack. Even if soldiers survive the war, they may have life-changing injuries that affect how they can function when back home.

We need to salute veterans who have sacrificed so much for us.

Post-traumatic stress disorder or PTSD

Post-Traumatic Stress Disorder affects 5 to 10 percent of people who have experienced a traumatic event (Bonanno, 2004). It is characterized by a constellation of symptoms that inhibit the healing process: flashbacks, over-reacting to situations, (e.g., a car backfiring may cause someone with PTSD to run for cover thinking the sound is a gun firing [Worden, 2009]), nightmares, insomnia, substance abuse, and aggressive behavior. Someone with PTSD may be so haunted by the death story that telling it gives her no relief. Instead, it may increase her anxiety and distress. She may do all that she can to avoid reminders of the traumatic event.

Parkes believes avoidance is impossible:

> …it is a paradox that, in order to avoid thinking about something, we have to think about it. That is to say, at some level, we remain aware of the danger that we are trying to avoid. Hence it should not surprise us if attempts at avoidance commonly fail. In sleep and at times of relaxed attention painful memories tend to float back into our mind and sufferers from PTSD find themselves reliving the trauma again (Parkes & Prigerson, 2010, p. 45).

If you think you may be suffering with PTSD, seek counseling. Dealing with the trauma of the death, and dealing with the grief of the loss may have to happen one after the other rather than concurrently in order for you to get relief. That is, you may first need to work through the symptoms of PTSD before you can grieve your loss. Throughout this book, I have talked about the benefits of telling your story and talking about your loss. For someone who is suffering from PTSD, talking about the loss may at first exacerbate the symptoms of PTSD.

It may take more time to accept the fact of a sudden death than it would take for an expected death. There are two things to face—the trauma of the event and your own grief.

If there was violence involved—intentional or not—this story needs to be told in a way that it can be eventually accepted. With violence, a complicating problem is that the images of the death are themselves hard to bear. You may need some relief from these images to slowly incorporate them into your life.

Managing the extreme grief of sudden loss

At first, the story may be too terrifying to tell or to think about. You cannot simply shut the door on an event. Nor can you let it consume your life so that you cannot function. You have to live between these extremes. There are many ways to manage this kind of grief.

Resilience

Resilience is the ability to moderate the amount of suffering that you can bear (Rynearson, 2010). If you break down and sob uncontrollably or act in a way that you normally wouldn't, such as an angry outburst, you need to then have a period of quiet and recovery. If you isolate yourself from others and feel sad and lost or maybe feel nothing, you can counterbalance that with an effort to reach out. If you experience flashbacks and act upon them, you can seek professional help to control them. If you experience terror attacks or panic attacks, you can experiment with different ways to calm yourself such as meditation, walks in nature, being in contact with loved ones, or seeking professional help. If you plan to carry out an act of retaliation or revenge, you can and must seek professional help so that you do not add to and multiply the suffering. All these counteractions are ways that you can build on or call on your resilience.

Stories that need to be told

Two stories need to be told: the story of the death and the story of the life.

The story of the death

Telling the story of the death is important. "Stories bring order into disorder and help us to bring meaning into a meaningless situation" (Gilbert, 2002, p. 224). It will take time to incorporate the story of a sudden loss into your life, especially if the death was violent.

Talk with your family and friends about it. Tell them the story. If you were present at the death, talk about what you saw. You may be surprised that telling the story is hard because everything happened so fast. In talking with your loved ones, this piecing together of the story, including writing it down, will help you as a group—whether family or friends—to remember together and to work the chronology into your lives. You may also be surprised at how natural it is to do—to get the chronology right—what happened, when, and possibly but not always, why. As human beings, we are storytelling beings. This chronology is something that you can all try to agree upon as the truth.

Whether the death is the result of natural causes, an accident, or violence, others may also be involved in the study of the chronology of events leading up to the death (the coroner, the doctor and other health care workers, police, the criminal justice system). Who was the last person to see your loved one alive? What did your loved one say to others? Were there signs or symptoms of impending trouble? What happened? Were there witnesses? Witnesses may be total strangers such as the nurse on a hospital unit, or another family member, or a friend, or you.

As you establish the chronology of events, your own individual story can be woven into the loss. Since each relationship is unique, each experience of grief is unique. Your story will be different from any other story, even if you are all in the same family. As an example, your loved one may have said the same thing to several people who heard those words at the same time you did. However, those words will have different meaning for each of the listeners because each listener's relationship with the deceased is different.

It may be hard for you to tell the story. If you were present at the death, you may regret that you were unable to help or to act to save your loved one's life. In a crisis, endorphins are released in the brain that can dull one's activity and reaction time. You may not have been able to help because of the chemical reactions that were occurring in your brain. This is also true for the dying person. The idea that your loved one may have died in terror and pain may haunt you. Endorphins are released in the dying person's brain, too. Sherwin Nuland (1994), surgeon and author, describes the protective nature of endorphins:

> Endorphin elevation appears to be an innate physiological mechanism to protect mammals and perhaps other animals against the emotional and physical dangers of terror and pain. It is a survival device, and because it has evolutionary value it probably appeared during the savage period of our prehistory when sudden life-threatening events occurred with frequency (p. 133).

I see it as the kindness of Mother Nature. You may be at fault for the death, for example, a car accident or an incident in war. Please get help so that you can tell and make sense of your story and move on in your life's journey. Although it is no consolation, one fear we share as human beings is that we will cause the death of another.

The story of the life

Although the image of your loved one's death may be frightening and haunting to you, as time goes by you will hopefully remember his entire life, not just the experience of his final moments, and the memory of your final interactions with him. "Slowly you can achieve a balanced image of the relationship and not blow out of proportion what was going on at the time of death," says Rando (2015, n.p.). Perhaps before your loved one died, you had a quarrel. The quarrel leaves you wishing you had said something different. Over time, you can slowly remember all the times that you were happy together. The one last quarrel does not negate all the good times. If you find that you cannot get beyond the death story to the life story, then it is a good time to seek help.

The journey toward meaning

For each person, this is different. It may be when you are in communion with nature that you discover meaning. It may be in assertiveness as you speak out to people who are insensitive to your needs. It may be in reaching out to others who have experienced a similar loss, giving and receiving help just by being together and listening to one another. It may be in searching for the meaning of your loved one's death. It may be discovering the meaning of your loved one's life. It may be in your working for justice so that others will live and not experience the same death as your loved one did. It may be in honoring the life of your loved one by taking the small step of just getting out of bed in the morning.

Hope

Everyone has to have a healthy dose of hope in order to make it through life. Without hope, life is meaningless, and we are stuck. After a sudden death, you may think and feel that your life as a survivor has no meaning. Your loved one's death may seem meaningless. You may be enveloped in despair, sadness, and anger.

But how do you achieve hope? Hope isn't always a permanent feeling. Hope is the small things that inspire you to go on—a moment of relief when someone smiles at you, the sounds of nature, a song you hear, or a poem you write. Please take note of these when they happen. They add up and help you to discover new meaning in your own life and celebrate your loved one's life.

Taking breaks

In Chapter 3, we talked about oscillation, going back and forth, between experiencing the pain of grief and going about other activities, including experiencing non-grief feelings and thoughts. At times oscillation happens naturally. At other times, you have to decide to oscillate, or take breaks. Here are some examples.

Take breaks from the story.

Telling the story of the death is the way you can make the fact of the death real, but in sudden death, it may be too real to comprehend and to accept. Retelling the story can exacerbate anxiety and horror. Take breaks from the story. Frank Ochberg helps people who are living with PTSD. He has written "Survivor's Psalm," which ends with these words: "I may never forget, but I need not constantly remember" (1993, p. 782).

Take breaks from life.

Perhaps you are invited to a wedding shortly after your spouse died, a children's sports event after your child died, or a play that is a tragedy, or a serious movie. You will have to decide if these events will be helpful to you or not. Be flexible for a while. If you accept an invitation to a party and are not sure you can take all that happiness but still want to connect with people, that is a conundrum. You might want to accept the invitation, knowing that you can change your mind even on the day when you are driving there. You might go to the party and soon realize, hey, this is not good. Then simply leave.

You may want to curtail your news consumption (TV, radio, or newspaper) for a while.

Try different ways of engaging: small groups with supportive people; a support group; large groups where you can be anonymous; engaging in your work where you have a specific role; volunteering in something where you won't think of your loved one, so you get some relief; or volunteering where you will think of your loved one and this will give you comfort and a sense of her presence. It is a process of trial and error—and effort. Engaging in life is good and healing. Being by yourself is good and healing. You need a balance of the two. Both are important and help you to grow on your grief journey.

Take breaks from social media.

Social media is a way to connect with others. You may feel lonely in your environment, and the Internet can be a place where you are rejuvenated and feel connected. There are websites where you can find information and support. Balance the Internet with actual people in your environment. The Internet can broaden your horizons and, ironically, it can also isolate you.

Grieving for a longer time than you expect

Grief is the age-old human collection of thoughts and feelings that help you to accept that your loved one has died and to move on in your life. With sudden death, you may find that each or all the tasks take longer to complete and that revisiting them becomes a common thing to do. Middle knowledge may occur more often when the death is sudden—forgetting that your loved one died and then remembering that, yes, she died.

The ever-present nature of grief

If you are living and loving, you will be losing and grieving. It is the way it is, the way of life. As time goes on there will be other losses that you will grieve. New losses can bring back memories of other losses, and you may experience more subsequent transient upsurges of grief (STUGs).

The intention to take it forward

Although your loved one is gone, you are here, and you can make a difference as you take forward what you have learned. Here are some intentions to take it forward after a sudden loss:

"From now on, I will tell people I love them. I won't just think it."

"From now on I will try to make my words kind and loving. I now never know when my last words will be to a fellow human being."

"If I have a disagreement with a loved one, I will try to resolve it before we part, or at least I will silently send him love on his way."

"From now on, I will love those who lose someone. I will be a compassionate presence in their life with cards, phone calls, emails, visits."

Working with your guilt feelings

These can range from imagined guilt to actual guilt. When death is sudden, there is no time to say you are sorry, to repair relationships, and to be there in your loved one's final moments. Remember you did the best that you could with the information that you had at the time. Try writing a letter to your loved one, sharing what you wished you had said or done.

Spending time in nature. Experiencing healing in nature.

Nature has a healing effect on the body and the mind. Take a daily walk in a natural environment. Do some gardening. Watch a sunrise. Watch a sunset.

Rejuvenating

Do something fun. Laugh with friends and family. Go on a fun trip or cruise. This is not escaping. You are connecting with others, and this gives strength.

Get some "i-Rest"

As described in other parts of the book, meditation is a powerful tool to relax and find inner peace. With a sudden loss, however, it is hard to quiet the mind. Psychologist Richard Miller (2015) created i-Rest (Integrative Restoration), a guided meditation, based on the ancient meditation practice called Yoga Nidra. Miller uses I-Rest to treat many populations, including soldiers who are living with PTSD. In i-Rest, both the "good" and the "bad" thoughts have a place. This integration of all thoughts and emotions honors the human experience, and takes the meditator to a state of peace, acceptance, and power.

If you have experienced a sudden loss, here are signs that may guide you to get extra help.

When to get help

You have symptoms of PTSD that will not go away: flashbacks, insomnia, depression, aggressive acts, anxiety, and fear.

You feel isolated and in despair and get no relief from these feelings. This can be a symptom of depression.

You are planning retaliation or revenge.

You have difficulty controlling your anger.

You are plagued by suicidal thoughts and have a plan as to how to commit suicide.

You find that you are abusing drugs or alcohol to control your thoughts and feelings.

Chapter Summary

In sudden loss, there is no preparation and no time to say good-bye. Even in a death that is expected there can be elements of the dying process that are sudden and traumatic.

Grieving a sudden loss has the same elements as grieving for an expected loss, yet it may take more time. When death is expected, you can prepare to say the things that need to be said and to do the things that need be done. Even if you are not present to do all that you would like to do, the dying person is on your mind. In a sudden death, you may not even be thinking of that person at all. You must start the grief process at point zero, with no preparation.

It is important to slowly appreciate the total life of the deceased and not only remember his final moments. Take breaks from your grief. Reach out to others for support. Spend time in nature. Seek counseling if the grief is too intense or you are experiencing symptoms of PTSD.

In sudden loss, the loss will always remain a part of your life even when you are feeling better. All loss changes us, sudden loss more so.

Julie Potter, MSW, LCSW

Chapter 12

Ambiguous Loss

"They say that the tree of loving grows on the bank of the river of suffering."
—Peter Yarrow, Singer

An ambiguous loss is one that is not complete and may keep changing. In death, the loss is completed, but an ambiguous loss continues to evolve.

Characteristics of ambiguous loss

Pauline Boss, a researcher and family therapist, created the term ambiguous loss. She was born in a farming community in Wisconsin. Her father and maternal grandmother were immigrants from Switzerland. Although they made lives for themselves in America, they and many others in the community missed their home country. Boss witnessed the melancholy feelings and homesickness in her family and in her town. She realized that the experience of this small immigrant community was a different kind of loss. People enjoyed their lives and missed their birth country. She called this an ambiguous loss and devoted her career to studying it and helping people to live with it.

Some examples of ambiguous loss:

> Your spouse may be living with Alzheimer's disease. The person you married is not the person who is with you now. Her decline continues and changes.

Your child went missing or as a soldier is missing in action. You live with the uncertainty: my son is probably dead, but I keep hoping that he is alive.

Your spouse is a workaholic, and when he comes home, he may relax with a beer, continue to work, and not participate in marital or family life. He is there, but he is not there.

Your friend is addicted to drugs. She is not the friend you knew. Her personality has changed. She and you are no longer interested in the same things.

You are an immigrant or a refugee who has left behind your homeland to live in a new place where you will be safe and have opportunities. At the same time, you grieve the loss of your country and wish you could return to your former life.

You have moved to a retirement community, giving up your home, which is filled with memories of your younger days. You grieve and yearn for a past that you cannot return to while at the same time learning about and enjoying your new place.

Our culture may not acknowledge or recognize an ambiguous loss and accept that it, too, deserves grief.

Yet the more we examine ambiguous loss, the more we may see that it manifests in our lives as the normal give and take of daily living. Your child goes to college, and you are sad that he does not stay in touch as much as you would like while at the same time, you are happy for him that he is on his way to adulthood. You are happy to be a member of a family. Yet, sometimes you think that you are more of an outlaw than an in-law, or you are sad that you are the black sheep.

Throughout your entire life, you are aging. Yet, there is a certain point when it is obvious that you are an older person. People may start holding doors for you and offering you seats on the bus. You may become ill. Beloved people around you also become ill and die at an alarming rate. The aging process continues to evolve in your body and brain. There are things that you used to do that are no longer possible for you. At the same time, you still feel young inside. Internally you feel you are beautiful and handsome, and you can jump, dance, run, see far into the distance, and sing. Becoming older is an ambiguous loss. We live with the paradox of the challenges and losses of old age and the youthful person living inside of us. These are some of the normal and, at times painful, conundrums we experience as human beings.

In addition, our modern mobile culture, which by its nature is in a state of change, seems to be fertile ground for ambiguous loss. We and our loved ones move to different places, change jobs, and go to school out of town. Our environment, without our permission, changes, too. Beloved landmarks, whether natural or manmade, disappear. When my sister was alive, she and her husband would frequently visit us and stay at a nearby motel. After my sister died, it gave me comfort to drive by that motel, and it brought back poignant memories. Then one day, I drove by the motel and saw that it had closed! Many months later, I drove by the same location and was saddened to discover that a new building was going up in its place.

Modernity brings change and opportunity in addition to sadness and grief, and ambiguous loss.

How to help with and live with ambiguous loss

As you learn about ambiguous loss, you may become more compassionate toward yourself and more compassionate toward others who may be living with a loss known only to them. Let's now consider things that may be helpful when faced with an ambiguous loss.

Be aware of the paradox of two things at once.

If you are experiencing an ambiguous loss, try to acknowledge its paradox. Something may be bad, and something may be good at the same time! Awareness of this paradox will help you to live in two worlds—the world of loss and the world of possibility. When you acknowledge the paradox in an ambiguous loss, you are not hopeless. Here are some examples of the paradoxes of ambiguous losses. You can make up your own. Also, since ambiguous loss changes, the paradoxes can change, too!

> My mother has Alzheimer's disease and she does not know who I am. Yet, she is still my mother, and I love her. I am learning new ways to relate to her.

My son has been missing in action for several years. He is probably dead. I have grieved his death, but I still have the hope that he is alive.

My "not here" spouse is painful to be with. I hope we can reconnect.

My friend is addicted to drugs. I miss who she was and now say hello to who she is.

I have emigrated to a new country. I will always hold my country of birth in my heart. I am learning to be in a new country and enjoy the challenges.

I have moved to a new neighborhood, school, retirement community, or nursing home. There is no going back. My memories sustain me during rough periods and also bring tears and grief.

Name the loss as an ambiguous loss.

It is important for you to name your loss and to tell your story as a loss that is evolving and ever present. Tell your story in whatever ways are available to you: talking with people who are understanding and compassionate, journaling, or creating spiritual or religious rituals.

When someone dies, the grieving person gets a lot of support. This is not necessarily true when someone is living with an ambiguous loss. An ambiguous loss may not even be recognized. You may be encouraged to look on the bright side, to think about people who are in worse situations, or to move on in your life and forget the past. Yet, ambiguous loss deserves your attention and your grief. By naming your loss as an ambiguous loss, you are validating the pain that you experience.

Find others who have a similar loss.

There are support groups that help people living with ambiguous loss: an Alzheimer's support group may provide a place for you to get help and support. You will also be able to share your experiences, which will be of help to others.

If you have moved to a new place, be on the lookout for people who are in a situation that is like yours, such as a new family who moves into your neighborhood. You can reach out and welcome them.

Expect your own ambivalent thoughts, feelings, and behavior.

A caregiver who is experiencing an ambiguous loss can have "love and hate for the same person, acceptance and rejection of their caregiving role, affirmation and denial of their loss" (Boss, 1999, p. 62). If your caregiver thoughts and feelings become completely negative, if you feel "burned out," then you may be a caregiver in trouble. Get respite from your caregiving role, if possible, by seeking help from others in carrying out your responsibilities. Consider getting counseling.

If you are anticipating a loss that could possibly be permanent, (your loved one goes off to war) you may hold your loved one at arm's length or quarrel with her to make the separation easier. Recognize these ambivalent feelings and behaviors. Forgive yourself for them. Reach out to your loved one in a caring way before the separation.

Do things that give you pleasure and that are stable in your life.

Cultivate activities in your life that give you pleasure: your place of worship, sports, time spent with supportive friends, and hobbies in your home environment that "take you away."

Act.

Ambiguous loss can also be a healthy signal that you have work to do in your relationship. Here are a few examples:

- learning skills so you can relate to someone living with dementia;
- initiating special remembrance rituals for someone who has gone missing;
- suggesting a vacation or a family event to involve the "not there" spouse;
- getting marital counseling;
- joining a support group; and
- pursuing addictions counseling.

Since ambiguous loss continues and evolves, it can take its toll on you, and you may not get relief from your grief. Here are some signs that may point toward needing extra help and support.

> **When to get help**
>
> Your sad thoughts and feelings are chronic and keep you from finding any enjoyment in life.
>
> Your grief is long standing and you continue to pine for your loved one.
>
> You feel burned out, tired and hopeless all the time.
>
> You cannot accept the paradox of two things at once—one painful, one hopeful. Although you may see the paradox, you cannot accept it into your life.
>
> You are angry a lot of the time about how your life has turned out.

Chapter Summary

An ambiguous loss is one that is not complete and keeps evolving. Your loved one may be living with a chronic evolving disease. Your loved one may have gone missing. Your partner may be there but not engaged with you. You may have moved to a new neighborhood, city, state, or country or changed jobs or schools. Your friend may be abusing alcohol or drugs and may be a different person from the one you knew in the past. In all these situations, the present may keep changing, and the loss is not final. In order to live with ambiguous loss, it is necessary to accept its paradoxes—to grieve for what was and to accept what is.

Reach out to people who understand your situation or who are in the same situation. Do things that give you pleasure or develop a hobby. Expect your own ambivalent thoughts, feelings, and behaviors in living with this kind of loss. Forgive yourself for your ambivalence. Take action and learn skills that will help you live with an ambiguous loss. It is possible to live in two worlds – the world of grief and the world of hope.

Chapter 13

Styles of Grieving

"Think and Feel."
—Carolyn Gichner, Aerobics Instructor

In her aerobics class, Carolyn Gichner instructs everyone to "Think and feel; think and feel" (personal communication, multiple occasions, 2000-2011). She wants each person to get the most out of the class by frequently checking in with herself: feeling the effects of the routine, thinking about what she is doing, and choosing the best way to participate in each moment. In this way, the class participants learn to take care of themselves during an inspiring and challenging class and avoid injury, too. The class participants do not just follow along. They use the class for their own growth and the development of their own power.

In grief, you may think more or feel more. Whatever you do more of, thinking and feeling are the bedrocks of being human. These are our basic skills, and they take us through life and grief. In this chapter, I will be discussing the five styles of grieving, as formulated by psychologists Kenneth Doka and Terry L. Martin (2010). I will also discuss personal characteristics and situations that may affect your style of grieving.

The five styles of grieving

Feeling style of grieving (Intuitive)

If you are a feeling griever, you may experience grief as waves of emotion and feelings washing over you. Reaching out to others and talking with others about your feelings is helpful to you. Interaction with others is important in your grieving.

Doka and Martin refer to this as Intuitive Grieving. Feeling has traditionally been associated with the feminine expression of the human species. In general but not always, women like to meet in groups and talk together. Men can also grieve in an intuitive way. In modern support groups, the feeling griever may enjoy the free-flowing sharing of feelings together. Just being in the company of others may be helpful.

Thinking and Doing style of grieving (Instrumental)

If you are a thinking and doing griever, you may experience mental and physical reactions: "I can't stop thinking about my loved one." "I go over my loss all the time in my mind." "Physically, it is like the wind has been knocked out of me." You may express your grief by doing something in memory of the person, e.g., planning a memorial or a ritual, building something, taking legal action. You may appreciate alone time, to process your grief and think about your loved one. You may talk to others about the life and accomplishments of your loved one.

Doka and Martin refer to this as Instrumental grieving. If this person joins a group, he appreciates a group that has a specific subject each time it meets. For him, action is important. We may traditionally identify this expression as more masculine in nature. If you ask him how he feels, he may say he feels fine, but his thoughts are full of grief. Women can also be Instrumental grievers.

Unrecognized grief (Disenfranchised)

You may have experienced a loss that is not recognized or accepted by others, and you may grieve intensely. Examples of possible unrecognized losses are a divorce, a job loss, a betrayal, relocation to a new place, an illness, changed physical or mental abilities. You may grieve over the death of a mentor, a friend, or a colleague. Your loss may be significant in your life, but others may not take your grief seriously. Any changes that you undergo, even positive changes, have elements of grief and loss. People may be impatient with your grief, may judge it, and may not even understand why you are grieving. After all, in many cases, no one died. Doka and Martin refer to this as Disenfranchised grieving.

One man describes the pain he experienced after his divorce and how it differed from the pain he had experienced after the death of his second wife:

> I have been married twice. My first wife left me, and I continued to raise our four children as a single father. Throughout those years, I became friends with Marie, who herself was divorced and was raising her children as a single mom. Ours was a platonic relationship for many years, and we provided mutual emotional and practical help to each other in raising our respective families.
>
> Then in our later years, once our family obligations were more complete, we fell in love and married. We both knew that Marie had had cancer and was in remission, and that it could happen again, which is exactly what happened. With this knowledge, I accepted whatever was going to happen. This resolve guided me throughout Marie's illness and death. During her illness, I grieved a lot as each day brought new losses, challenges and many poignant moments. Her grave illness was a burden for her, her family and for me, too. When Marie died, I felt relief both for her that she was not suffering and for myself that the journey was over. I had made it. I had been able to provide Marie with the care she needed.
>
> I made it through two losses—the divorce from my first wife and the death of my second wife. Ironically, I had been in more pain from the divorce than from Marie's death. With the divorce, I was angry with God. How could this happen when I was doing everything right? I was angry with my friends, who barely acknowledged what I was going through. I was angry with my first wife whose actions changed my life.
>
> With Marie, we both knew the cancer might return. We were as prepared as we could be for this. We loved each other, and we went through it together.
>
> —Stephen Paddack

Even your way of grieving may disenfranchise you from others, maybe even from yourself. You may judge yourself: "Why aren't I crying?" or

"Why am I crying so much?" The Thinking and Doing griever may be judged early on that she isn't grieving: Someone might wonder: "Why aren't you crying?" And later in grief, the feeling griever may be judged: "Aren't you over this yet? Why are you still crying?"

Secret or hidden grief (Dissonant)

This person cannot express his or her experience of grief. You may be a man for whom crying is healing, but you cannot cry in front of others (Doka & Martin, 2010). Others may judge you negatively for crying. You may be a woman who wants to be alone with her grief, but others may interpret this as a rejection. You may be in the company of others but cannot grieve with them. Doka and Martin refer to this as Dissonant grieving.

Author Joyce Carol Oates (2013) recalls the hidden grief of her mother. Her maternal grandfather, probably a violent person, and quick to anger, was murdered in a tavern fight, leaving his family of a wife and eight children destitute. Oates' mother was given away to relatives who raised her. Oates recalls:

> I was well into adulthood by the time my mother's secret heritage came to light, and even then it was a faint, glimmering light, which no one could acknowledge without averted eyes. My mother's account of that traumatic time in her early life centered not on the murder of her father, whom she had not known, but on the mortifying fact of having been "given away." My mother, who had always been a happy woman, generous, warm, and kind, much loved by family and friends, was eighty years old when she told me the story, repeating over and over, as though no time had passed since the trauma of 1917, "My mother didn't want me. I used to cry and cry" (n.p.).

Blended grieving style

Grief is a thinking and feeling process (Rosenblatt, 1996). It is an outer and an inner process and an active and a passive process. Sometimes, we can share this process with others. Sometimes, we need to be alone with it. Sometimes, we have to hide it from others. Whether we cry out, reach out, go inside, withdraw, or hide, these are all part of the human expression. You do not have to think or feel anything is wrong with you, and that you are not grieving "perfectly." Grief is a powerful and natural process. I encourage you to go along with your own thinking and feeling process.

Most of us are Blended grievers. Whoever we are, we have to feel safe if we are to share our grief with others. Women, and many men, generally reach out to one another in their grief. Being in a trusted group helps them to feel safe. Men, and many women, generally do not enjoy or feel comfortable in groups. Being in solitude for a time is safer.

Our culture is biased toward the person who feels her grief. However, as you can see, there is a wide variety of grief styles.

Factors that affect your grief style or expression

Other factors can affect how you will express your grief: your personal grief history, gender, culture, your age when you experience a loss, how accepted and loved you feel, how safe you feel, and the amount of community involvement in the loss. Let's look at some of these factors now.

Your age

By the time you are in your sixties, you will probably have experienced many losses: the death of parents, relatives and friends, retirement or job loss, health and mobility losses.

Despair and loneliness may be the challenges that older people face when they experience losses. For younger adults, who have the promise of a long life ahead, anger and rage may be their challenges when faced with a loss. This is not to imply that these will be the only emotions experienced.

For children, who are dependent on their parents, yearning and safety may be their challenges. The closer their attachment is to the adult who dies (parent, grandparent, sibling), the more they may grieve. They will appreciate reassurance that they will be taken care of by caring adults in their life. Their grief may continue intermittently throughout their lives with each milestone of their development. At turning points in their lives, there will be opportunities to revisit their loss.

Children may be openly sad and need emotional support—and then go outside to play. Play is how children learn and process important life events. For teens, peers are a way to establish their own identity and comfort zone. It isn't any wonder then that in grief they gravitate to their peers for support.

Your personal history

Each one of us brings with us a personal history of grief. When my mother died in her eighties, I remember my heartbroken father saying, "Well, I guess I will have to get used to going to funerals now." At the time, I was in my 40's, had moved out of town, and had attended some, but not many, funerals. It amazed me that Papa, as an older man, had not gone to many funerals! Growing up, I do not remember attending funerals. So, as a young adult, I was consequently in a fog when it came to death and funerals.

Not so for others. In war-torn areas of the world, people of all ages witness daily violence and death. The African American, Native American, and immigrant communities have experienced racism and loss in myriad forms for generations—violence, trauma, premature death, inadequate or minimal medical care, and incarceration. Death and funerals are all too common, starting at a very young age.

Your upbringing and early experiences influence your grief expression, sometimes making it more difficult, sometimes easier. Grief may touch places in you that you thought you were finished with, places that are new to you, places that are wounded, and places that are familiar to you. What you can do is to be aware of your past and honor it as you grieve in the present.

Sense of safety, acceptance, validation, and love

Do you feel safe? Do you feel accepted? Do you feel validated? Do you feel loved? When we grieve, we are in a new territory and, quite naturally, seek safety.

You may feel safe when your grieving energy is contained in some way—through ritual, song, writing, poetry, meditation, prayer, a remembrance activity, talking with a trusted friend, reading a book, or a moment of silence. Tom Golden, clinical social worker and therapist says, "The word 'container' is meant to describe anything that allows us to move from an ordinary state of awareness into the experience of pain, and then lets us move out of the pain again" (Golden, 2000, p. 135). Try it: light a candle in honor and memory of your loved one and sit with it for a few minutes. Journal about what you are experiencing. Then you can go back to your regular life.

You may feel safe in a group, or when you can retreat to solitude. According to psychologist, Shelley Taylor (2002), many women may feel safer when they reach out to others for support, acceptance, and love. Many men may feel safer when they are alone, and when their aloneness is respected. "Keep in mind that Jesus, like Moses and Buddha, when in need, would head for the desert and spend long periods there alone. I don't remember Mary or Martha telling him he needed to join a support group and talk about things. No, they let him be, and honored his intuitive wisdom" (Golden, 2013, p. 40). Men may work on a grief-related project either alone or with others, and in that context, will be more comfortable sharing their grief experience. Grief projects can be a memorial of some kind, or even legal action to rectify a situation related to the death.

Does this mean that if you are group-oriented, you will stay in a group? Or if you are alone-oriented, you will stay alone? No. This simply means that initially you will gravitate toward where you feel the safest before you can venture beyond your comfort limits. "None of us, when we are in distress, is inclined to do what is unfamiliar or uncomfortable," says Chaplain Daniel Duggan (2014, p. 45).

Gender

In many cultures around the world, gender roles in grief are set by social custom. A woman grieves one way, and a man grieves another way. The dual grieving ways create a unified communal grief expression—an expression in which the entire community feels safe, accepted, validated, loving, and loved. Western culture is diverse, and we cannot categorize a male and female style of grieving. However, women tend to reach out to others for support and understanding in their grief. Men are more likely to initially retreat into solitude to process their grief.

A woman may need to be understood. This is not necessarily so for a man. He may simply want to be heard (Duggan, 2014).

I recommend the following three books that address men's grief: *Men, Grief and Solitude* by Daniel Duggan, *Swallowed by a Snake* by Tom Golden, and *Men and Grief* by Carol Staudacher. Whatever your gender, these books give a broader understanding of the grief process and may help you to accept your own individual grief expression.

Even if you are more comfortable alone, you still need the support and kindness of others. In the instance of infant or child death, many men feel left out. Their wives receive attention and support while their grief as a father is bypassed or given scant attention (Staudacher, 1991). Even if you are more comfortable in a group, you can benefit from alone times—reading, journaling, remembering, watching a sunset, or visiting the cemetery.

Normally we think when someone is grieving that she looks sad, she talks to others about how she is feeling, and she may cry. That is only one manifestation, the easiest one for us to relate to in our culture.

Table 13.1 delineates gender-related differences. These differences are quite fluid. Whatever your gender, you will probably see aspects of yourself on both sides of the table. In less diverse cultures and in some religions, gender roles are more or less set. Our modern culture is more diverse, and our gender roles and grief styles are continually changing. It is fortunate that many genders, formerly often excluded, are now recognized: homosexual, bisexual, transgender, and queer. Table 13.1 separates men and women. I would like to add the words *feminine expression* and *masculine expression*, which include all genders.

Table 13.1 Gender-related differences in relationships[1]	
Women (feminine expression)	Men (masculine expression)
Rapport or feeling talk	Report talk
Sharing feelings and relationships	Storytelling: who, what, when, where, how, and why
Wants to be listened to and understood	Wants to have their story witnessed; doesn't need to be understood
Egalitarian or flat in their social structure	Hierarchical
Handles several goals at once and has a broader perspective	Keeps to one goal or task and is more narrowly focused
Relational/being-oriented	Task/doing-oriented
Tends toward the nurturer, co-creator role identity	Tends toward the provider, protector/warrior, progenitor/creator role identity
"Connected" identity	"Separate" identity
Moves into relationships to cope	Moves inward to cope

1 Duggan, D. R., *Men, Grief and Solitude*, (Solitude Publishers, LLC, Alexandria, VA, 2014), p. 48.

Community involvement in loss

In natural disasters, terrorist attacks such as 9/11, and assassinations of public figures, we come together to grieve as a community and experience the power of the community with an outpouring of love, financial support, rituals, memorials, and change (hopefully for the better). The human spirit can be at its best in these times, and the unity experienced is natural and real, albeit short-lived.

Sadly, not every group gets attention and love in community disasters. Many tragedies are recognized but do not unify us. Hurricane Katrina, for example, severely damaged the community of New Orleans due to the lack of help. The city continues to heal from the callous treatment its citizens received.

Chapter Summary

The five ways we grieve are called our grief styles or grief expressions:

Feeling style (Intuitive) – This griever reaches out to others and may benefit from a group experience. She shares her feelings of grief. Grief is a feeling experience.

Thinking style (Instrumental) – This griever thinks about his loss, plans memorial activities, retells the events of the loss. Grief is experienced in a physical and thinking way. This griever may also appreciate alone time.

Unrecognized grief (Disenfranchised) – This griever experiences a loss that is not appreciated or accepted by others, thus gets minimal or no support and understanding.

Secret grief (Dissonant) – This griever, for whatever reason—cultural, familial or job expectations—cannot express his grief.

Blended grieving style – By and large, we are all blended grievers—sometimes thinking, sometimes feeling, sometimes doing, sometimes planning, sometimes withdrawing, and sometimes reaching out.

Other factors influence your grief expression: your age; your personal grief history; how safe, accepted, and loved you feel; your gender; and the community's response to your loss.

Knowing about the different grieving styles and factors that affect them helps us to accept ourselves in our grief journeys and others in their grief journeys.

Part 4
GUIDES TO UNDERSTANDING

Part 4 includes concise guides to the grief experience: tips and validations, danger signs to watch for, and how to help.

Julie Potter, MSW, LCSW

Chapter 14

Grief Guide: Tips and Validations

> *"I've developed a new philosophy—*
> *I only dread one day at a time."*
> —*Charles M. Schulz*

This chapter provides tips to make it through each day, and to validate your experiences. As stated frequently in this book, grief is a powerful experience. You can participate in its power by using your own power to experience it and direct its course or by surrendering to its power. Using your power and surrendering are both important. Swimmers instinctively learn when they can swim, when they can dive into a huge wave, and when they can ride the wave. It is trial and error, and eventually inner knowledge and wisdom are attained, with tumbles and falls, and mouthfuls of sand along the way.

Simply scroll through the topics to give yourself a boost. Or stop at one or two of them to read completely. Grief is natural to us as human beings. It may not feel good, but it is good. It is a good process. It is a powerful process.

Each loss is unique.

Each relationship is unique. Each grief is unique. You may grieve one loss deeply, yet another loss will have little effect on you. Even in the same family, you may experience the loss more deeply or less deeply than the others.

Sometimes you will feel okay, sometimes terrible.

You may be happy that you have gotten through grief and are sailing along quite well when a reminder comes up and you seem to sink back into grief. Grief has been described as a spiral, where you are progressing upward on the spiral. Although you are making progress, you continually come back to a similar position on the spiral (but higher); it is at these times that grief responses may return.

Reminders are plentiful and painful.

As time goes on, reminders can lessen in frequency and intensity. However, reminders will happen for the rest of your life, and your reaction to them may change. You may have a STUG (Subsequent Transient Upsurge of Grief). You may eventually welcome STUGs. These are opportunities to reminisce, remember, and to be grateful. STUGs tell us that the person who died is important to us and to others.

Talk about your loss to as many sensitive people as you can.

Telling your story helps you to accept the reality of what has happened and to get the story straight in your mind and in your heart. If you confide in a loved one who is grieving the same loss, this may help. However, a fellow griever may disagree with your story. He is a different person. His relationship with the deceased is different, and consequently his story is different. You may talk about an event that gave you comfort, whereas that same event may have brought suffering or ambivalence to a fellow griever. Accept your story and respect the stories of others.

It takes courage to be yourself and to tell your inner truth to others. The tendency, when not understood or heard, is to recoil, to lose trust in others. Don't give up. Continue looking for sensitive souls with whom to talk about your loss.

If your family or friends do not want to hear your story, there are support groups, volunteers, and therapists who can help. Remember, you can also talk to yourself in the form of journaling, artistic expression, making a memorial to your loved one.

As you grow and change, your story will grow and change with you. Even if you have told your story many times to others and to yourself, each time you may gain a deeper appreciation for your loved one.

Talk to your deceased loved one.

This is a way to keep the memory of your loved one alive. As your life goes on, your relationship goes on too. A death has happened, but the relationship does not end. It changes. You do not have to use language to talk to your loved one. Silence is the language of the heart.

Think.

It is natural to think about your loved one—the memories you shared, the conflicts you had, some resolved, some not. It is natural that you will think about your loved one as you go through the rooms in your house and the streets in your town. Every place has many reminders and many memories. It is natural to think about events leading up to the death and then the death and to think about the entire relationship. Each part of your relationship is included in the loss. In time, thinking about your loved one will bring healing and joy.

Also, think about your grieving process. Thinking about it will lead you to greater understanding of the process as you are experiencing it and will better inform your choices of how to direct the process.

Stop thinking.

Grief takes a lot of energy. Take a break from your grief. Go for a swim, a walk, a run, a jog. Rent a movie. Call a friend. Go to a museum. Meditate. Walk barefoot on your lawn in the rain, or in the morning when there is dew on the grass—a good mood elevator. Take "thinking breaks."

Take good care of yourself.

Grief is stressful and can compromise your immune system. You are at greater risk for illness when you are grieving. Have regular medical checkups, get as much rest as you can, eat well, avoid the overuse of addictive substances, do some exercise, meditate/pray/attend religious services, and reach out to others who have experienced a similar loss. Do something fun: a movie, a play, a sports event on TV or at a park.

If someone asks you to take on a new task, you may have little choice but to do it when job related. However, there are times when you can give yourself time to decide: "I'll get back to you." "I need to think about that."

Commune with nature.

Someone once told me that we feel good in nature because of its energy. The fresh air, bright colorful flowers, trees, the wind, a blue lake, a muddy river, the sun in all its manifestations – these things help us to feel good because something energetically is happening within us when we are in nature. The feeling of seeing a picture of a river is entirely different from being at the river.

Weep.

You may weep in sorrow and gain healing. You may weep in anger and find that your anger softens. You may weep in frustration when nothing is going right and find relief.

Write.

Writing helps to slow down the mind and focus your thoughts. When anxiety and fear reign in the middle of the night, take out pen and paper, and write. Write freely and without reserve. No one has to see what you have written.

Some writing ideas:

- Write about what you are thinking.
- Write about what you are feeling.
- Write different kinds of lists to help you feel confident, powerful and in charge ("to do" lists, problem-solving lists).
- Write about how you are doing.
- Write a letter to your deceased loved one – a letter of love, a letter of anger, a letter of guilt and sorrow, a sad letter, a happy, light-hearted letter.
- Write a letter from your deceased loved one to you.

Forgive yourself.

Be gentle with yourself. In the grieving process, you may say or do things that you later regret. Forgive yourself and move on. The Talmud says, "One must forgive everything one does in his grief."

In the caregiving process, you may say or do things that you later regret. Forgive yourself and move on. One must forgive everything one does in the caregiving process.

In life, you may say or do things that you later regret. Forgive yourself and move on. One must forgive everything one does in life.

Forgive others.

Our human relationships are filled with trial and error. Forgive those who do not appreciate what you are going through or who try to help in an unhelpful way. There will be others whom you won't want to forgive. That's okay. Trust in the power of time to guide you.

You may believe that the very person who needs your forgiveness is your deceased loved one. Do not make forgiveness of others, and of your deceased loved one, a top priority. Take care of yourself first. If over time, your anger and dissatisfaction with others inhibits your functioning, then it may be time to visit forgiveness.

Educate the helper.

People want to help you but may be afraid that they will say the wrong thing—and they very well might. Their silence does not necessarily mean that they don't care. Break the ice by mentioning the name of your loved one. Gently let them know when something is not helpful.

They may say, "Don't cry." You can say, "These tears help me and are part of grief."

They may give you advice and their advice may be helpful. If it is not helpful, you can say, "The most helpful thing in the world would be for you to simply listen to me or give me a hug."

They may want to offer support and open the conversation of grief. This may be helpful. If not, you can say, "Right at this moment, I would just like to enjoy your company, but I am grateful to you for reaching out to me. There will be other times when I would like to talk about my loss, but not right now."

Reach out to people.

Be around people who accept you and bring out the best in you. Time and again, bereaved people have told me that out of the blue, they will meet new people who will be very helpful to them whereas their own friends and family fall short. (Family and friends may also be grieving, or they may have expectations and a timetable for your grief).

If friends come into your life, enjoy them. Enjoy and be on the lookout for the small human interactions. Sometimes, a smile from a stranger will be the pick-me-up that helps you through the day.

Create these interactions, too. If you reach out in a light-hearted way, you may be rewarded with a smile or a conversation.

Avoid certain people.

It is okay to avoid people with whom you feel annoyed or uncomfortable. We all have those "certain people" in our lives, who in the best of circumstances rub us the wrong way. There will be times when you will feel in a better position to see them again.

Be wary.

Remember, you are in a vulnerable time of your life, and there are people out there who may take advantage of you financially and emotionally.

Say an inner thank-you.

You may feel that you have absolutely nothing to be grateful for. However, saying an inner thank-you is a heart-opener. It helps you to see what is around you and what is in you. It helps you to connect with the world and all the beings in it. Try it often. Gratitude gives you inner power.

Start a gratitude journal, and every day write down things that you are grateful for. You may find that as time goes on, there are many things that you are grateful for.

Laugh.

If you laugh and have a good time, you may feel that you are dishonoring your loved one. This is not so. Laughter helps your immune system, releases an abundance of endorphins in your body, and helps to relieve stress. Laughter does not mean that you will forget your loved one. No. You will always remember. Laughter helps these remembrances to be light-hearted.

Expect former losses to resurface in your life.

Whenever we go through a loss in our lives, we may re-experience grief from former losses. In addition, old patterns of behavior and forgotten insecurities, dating back to your childhood and adolescence, can come up. There were times in childhood and adolescence when you may have been insecure and didn't know who you were. Grief brings up these feelings. You don't have to be a child to feel like one. You don't have to be a teen to feel like one.

Have faith in the grief process.

It is natural. It is powerful. It is human, and people have been doing it throughout the ages.

Look for meaning. Create meaning.

Look for meaning in your life and in the death of your loved one. You can discover meaning by making up rituals, telling stories and listening to stories about your loved one, praying for guidance and support, or joining a support group where you can be with people who have experienced a similar loss.

Create rituals.

Commonly accepted rituals are the funeral, graveside service, and memorial service—powerful community rituals that unite the community in the grief experience.

Try making up a ritual of your own. It can be simple—lighting a candle and being silent for a time, visiting the cemetery.

Resolve your guilt.

Guilt is in the mind. Sorrow and remorse are in the heart. Come out of your mind, and go into your heart again and again. Where there is remorse, there is humility, and you can change your behavior. Guilt alone won't change anything.

Read.

For many, reading helps. For others, reading is a chore. A short book (78 pages) called *A Guide for the Bereaved Survivor* by Bob Baugher

(2013) is helpful and accessible to just about everyone. Each even-numbered page explores a grief reaction. On the facing odd-numbered page are suggestions for dealing with that reaction. Say you are experiencing guilt, turn to the guilt page where you will learn about guilt plus useful suggestions.

Many people read grief memoirs, stories by people who have experienced grief. There are self-help books such as this one and books completely unrelated to grief that may touch a chord in you—short stories, essays, novels, and poems.

Here are additional books that many have found to be helpful:

- *A Grief Observed* by C.S. Lewis
- *The Year of Magical Thinking* by Joan Didion
- *Being Mortal* by Atul Gawande
- *How to Survive the Loss of a Love,* by Harold H. Bloomfield, M.D., Melba Colgrove, Ph.D., and Peter McWilliams
- *Living when a Loved One has Died,* by Earl A. Grollman

Seek help.

When you find that the roller coaster of grief emotions is too overwhelming, help is out there for you. It can be a volunteer, a clergy, a family member, a support group, a chaplain, a neighbor, a book, a pet, a friend, or a website. If that help is insufficient, seek professional help.

If you are considering harming yourself by suicide, or harming others by homicide, revenge, or retaliation, seek professional help immediately.

If your primary antidote to the pain of grief is alcohol or drugs, seek professional help.

If you are depressed, anxious, or angry most of the time, seek professional help.

Chapter Summary

The above tips and validations may be helpful to you. They are suggestions, and only you will know what is best for you.

We love each person in a unique way. We grieve for each person in a unique way. Grief is as natural and as unique as love. Grief is a form of love.

Harnessing the Power of Grief

My wish for you is that you will experience your grief in your own way, and not judge yourself. Try not to look for trends: Oh, I'm getting better. Oh, I'm getting worse. Simply take a day at a time and try not to get discouraged. If you do get discouraged, read this chapter again for a pick-me-up. Or read Chapter 15, "Danger Guide: Danger Signs to Watch for."

Julie Potter, MSW, LCSW

Chapter 15

Danger Guide: Danger Signs to Watch For

> *"This is not the time to 'be brave.'*
> *In fact, it takes great courage to ask for help."*
> —*Harold H. Bloomfield, psychiatrist and author*

Grief is a lonely process. When your sad feelings become an unremitting depression, when negative emotions such as anger, anxiety, and fear are constant in your life, or when a sense of the futility of life turns into suicidal thoughts and plans, it is time to get help as soon as possible.

When grieving, you are more vulnerable to unscrupulous or insensitive people. Your normal defenses are down. You may fall in love with the wrong person or make snap decisions that are later regretted such as selling property, giving away possessions, or moving. There may be times when it is hard to sort all this out.

If you are experiencing any of the following, consider talking with a mental health professional, chaplain, or spiritual mentor, joining a support group, or getting a legal or financial consultation:

You have no respite from your grief. After a few years, it continues to feel as if it just happened, and your grief reactions continue to be intense.

You have a history of mental health challenges. Examples include depression and anxiety disorders. These can be intensified during grief.

You have experienced many losses. This new loss can bring all of them back.

Your anger is extreme. It is hard for you to control angry outbursts, and you lash out verbally and/or physically at others. You are planning acts of retaliation and revenge.

You engage in risky behaviors. Examples include substance abuse, such as alcohol and drugs; unprotected sex; or sex with multiple partners.

You are experiencing a high level of anxiety. You are fearful of leaving your home or meeting new people. You are fearful of being in the company of people with whom you are normally comfortable such as family, friends, and colleagues.

You feel betrayed by people who you thought were trustworthy. They may have taken advantage of you financially and emotionally, cheating you out of your financial resources or entering into a bogus romantic or friend relationship with you.

You feel a sense of isolation and lack of self-confidence. The guilt and/or shame that you are experiencing keep you from participating fully in life and regaining a sense of self-confidence.

You feel guilty about something you did or failed to do. You have caused, or think you could have prevented, someone's injury or death, through willfulness or negligence, or as part of your job in the medical profession, a police force, or the military.

You have suicidal thoughts. These thoughts will not go away, and you have a plan as to how you will commit suicide.

You feel depressed all the time. You have a continual sense of doom. You feel bitter about life, and do not experience any joy or hope. Life is meaningless to you all the time.

You are experiencing symptoms of Post-Traumatic Stress Disorder (PTSD), These symptoms are described in Chapter 11. Joyce Boaz, Director of Gift from Within, a website dedicated to PTSD education and support, defines PTSD in this way: "The body's alarm system gets stuck in the 'on' position, causing sensations of fear, anticipation of doom, unwanted recollection of terrible events, and a loss of the ability to fully experience the emotions of love and joy" (2014, n.p.).

You find that most of the time you are lonely. You may feel cut off from others emotionally and/or physically, at a time when connection with others could be helpful and healing.

Others do not know about your loss, for example, the death of a friend or lover. Others may not appreciate your loss, such as leaving your home and moving to a new geographical area.

There is no one with whom you can express what you are going through. You may not have family or friends who you feel are sympathetic to you, and who will listen.

You may experience one or more of the above things at one time or another. In and of themselves, they are part of the human experience.
The questions are:

- How long lasting are they in your life?
- Can you find ways to compensate for them, go through them, and go beyond them?
- Or are you stuck?
- Is your quality of life diminished and even at risk because of them?
- If your answer to the last two questions is yes, then please consider getting some extra help.

Finally, you may be doing fine, but a member of your family or your friend is struggling. Reach out to them and suggest counseling.

Where to go for help.

For immediate help, go online and look for crisis hotlines. Different areas of the country have specific numbers.
If there is an immediate or imminent crisis, call 911.
Call your local hospice, which may provide bereavement counseling and knows bereavement and counseling resources in your community.

Talk to someone from your religious group. Many religious groups have bereavement programs and community outreach programs.

Some useful resources:

- **Substance Abuse**
  - Alcoholics Anonymous www.aa.org
  - Al-Anon, for people who are worried about someone with a drinking problem. www.al-anon.org
  - NIAA-NIH National Institute on Alcohol Abuse and Alcoholism www.niaaa.nih.gov
  - Drug Abuse: Medline-Plus. medlineplus.gov/drugabuse.html

- **Hospice**
  - Hospice Foundation of America www.hospicefoundation.org

- **Mental Health**
  - NAMI, The National Alliance on Mental Illness Helpline 800-950-NAMI www.nami.org

- **Suicide**
  - National Suicide Prevention Hotline 1-800-273-8255 (available 24 hours every day)

Chapter 16

Help Guide: How to Help

"This is part of the task of friends—to help keep the memory of loved ones alive, to show concern for one another, particularly when someone has suffered a great loss."
—Reverend Granger E. Westberg

When you have come through the journey of grief, you have acquired knowledge and developed wisdom. You may then wish to help others. Before you help others, first go through your own process of grief. When you come to a place of comfort in your grief, when you are more at ease in your day-to-day life and grief is not a constant intense experience in your life, then that may be a good time to reach out to help others either informally or in a volunteer program.

For now, your job is to grieve and heal. Read this chapter, and then wait a year or so, and read it again.

How to help

Newly widowed spouses would frequently tell me how insensitive their family, friends and colleagues were. Then, there would be a pause, and they might say, "Yes, I was like that, too. I did not know how hard grief was. Now, I know." To respect the grief of others is truly enough. You are helping others by having respect for their experience.

A chaplain who was supervising students and volunteers used to say, "When you are helping someone, remember, you are entering a sacred space." Enter that space with humility. Leave your answers at the door.

Leave your fear at the door. Leave your wish to "get it right" at the door. Enter with humility.

When you are visiting with a newly bereaved friend or loved one, put your phone on silent. If you are having a phone conversation, turn off the TV, shut down your computer and other devices so that you will not be distracted and you will be present. Set aside an amount of time that you can commit to so that you will not be in a hurry or interrupted. Here are some practical ways to do this:

Be present. Don't let your mind wander. Be focused on your visit.

Ask a good question. In order to honor a person's experience, instead of asking, "How are you feeling?" try asking, "What is the toughest thing about your loss?" (Golden 2000, p. 161) "How is it going for you today?" In this way, you open the door for both thoughts and feelings. The question "How are you?" is more of a "hello" than an actual question seeking an answer.

Listen, listen, listen, rather than immediately responding, which is what most of us do. Try taking a deep breath before responding, or count silently to 5, or 10, or 20. When everyone else has something to say, can you be the one to simply be present?

Welcome silence. Enjoy the silence between you and the grieving person and have faith that she is using these quiet moments to simply be in your company in her grief.

Avoid "me too" comments. This is not the time for your story. This is the time for the grieving person's story.

Do not try to fix it. That is not your job. We are always trying to do something to make things better. Accept that your efforts to fix someone's grief, or make it better do not help. Just be there and listen.

Give space to the griever. Try not to take the griever's roller coaster of emotions personally. If the grieving person seems impatient with you, give him time and space. If he changes the subject, let the subject be changed.

Keep the lines of communication open. Reach out to the griever. The grieving person may simply be trying to keep things together and will not want to talk with you or visit with you. Accept that your overture may or may not be reciprocated. However, it will be remembered.

Don't rely on appearances. Just because someone does not look like they are grieving, don't jump to the conclusion that everything is okay, and that things are back to normal.

Mention the deceased person's name. Reminisce about your own memories and experiences with the deceased. Grieving people mention how wonderful it is to hear these memories, and to share their own memories.

Do not set a timetable for grief. The intense grief process can be short, and it can be long too. An undercurrent of grief can last a whole lifetime.

Don't tell people not to feel what they are feeling, or not to think what they are thinking. You may be trying to reassure the grieving person, or you may simply be tired of hearing the story again and again. Your attempts to reassure and/or your impatience may be closing the door on the griever's opportunity to experience the pain of grief.

Listen to the story. Telling the same story is an important element in grief. Your listening to the story helps with this process. Expect and encourage repetition of the story.

Send notes, texts, or emails to the griever. Let her know you are thinking about her.

Give advice sparingly. When the griever asks your advice, answer to the best of your ability. Remember, your answer may not help. You can ask him what others have suggested to him and did he find others' advice helpful? You can ask him what his answers are too.

Do not judge the griever's experience. Honor and respect it. Remember, it is his experience, not yours.

Persevere in your efforts. We all want to help, but we do not want to pester anyone either. And that stops us from doing anything, which is not helpful. So, have the intention to help, and reach out. Use this list of helping ideas to guide you.

Forgive yourself. If you make mistakes in helping, learn from them, and move on. Have compassion for yourself. You are doing something courageous in helping another human being.

Reach out, especially when someone comes to mind. Don't wait for too long or put it off, waiting for the appropriate moment. The appropriate moment is when the person has come to your mind. Make a plan when that person has come to mind. When my brother-in-law who lived out of town was diagnosed with cancer, I thought I would visit him when his treatments were finished. I never got there. He died during the course of his treatment. After that, I decided that I would reach out no matter what. When my sister, who also lived out of town, got cancer, I sent weekly notes, emails, and called her on the phone frequently. We worked out many times that we could be together during the four years that she was ill.

Reach out on anniversary days. This includes the death date, birthday, and special remembrance days.

Reach out on holidays. There are eight national holidays in the U.S. That's eight opportunities to reach out, in addition to days such as Mother's Day, Father's Day, and various other religious and community holidays. Reach out with a card, an email, a text greeting, a phone call, and the best—your presence. Make a date to be together during the holidays.

Don't give up on your friendship. Grief changes a person. Can you stand by your new and changed friend? Many changes may not be for the better. You have to decide what is more important, your wish that your friend could be the "old you" or your friendship. The grieving person may find new friends who "get it" when you may not. This is okay, and you may just have to accept this. Be happy for your friend, and keep the door of your friendship open, too.

Plan fun activities together. You could go on a walk; take in a movie; meet for coffee, tea, or a meal; go fishing; or play some pick-up basketball.

Be on the lookout for ways that you can be helpful. You could run errands, provide transportation, etc.

Respond to dangerous ideas. If the grieving person seems in deep despair and talks about suicide, ask this question: "Do you have a plan on how you will commit suicide?" If the answer is "yes," tell your friend to get help, or better yet, assist your friend in getting help. If the suicide seems like an imminent plan, call a Crisis Hotline, or a Suicide Prevention Hotline immediately. A grieving person may say, "If I were to die today, I wouldn't care. I would be happy that my life would be over." Actually, we all may feel like that at times. The point is, is the grieving person having a down day, or is she suicidal? Don't be shy. It is very important that you explore this issue. "Are you planning to commit suicide?" If the grieving person responds to you with incredulity, "What, are you crazy?" just be relieved.

Set boundaries. If the grieving person seems to be asking for too much time with you, you can set a time limit for your visit, and then stick to it. If you feel burdened by your visit, this is a sign to shorten it so that you will have energy for your time together. Consider an hour as a good guideline. Be aware that the grieving person may not have a lot of energy, so limiting your time together can make it a good experience for both of you.

Keep your conversations with the grieving person confidential. We are members of many communities where people know one another or know of one another. If you share confidential information with others about the grieving person, even if you don't mention the person's name, others may easily put two and two together and will know who you are talking about. Keeping sensitive information confidential is a good idea, and good manners. The exception to this is if the grieving person is a danger to himself or to others. Then it is imperative for you to disclose confidential information about the griever to a professional.

Chapter Summary

All of these "helping ideas" are no more than good manners. And if in our daily relationships we use the same care as we do with those who are grieving, we can't go wrong. Human relationships are a process of trial and error, so, sure, we will make mistakes. But hopefully we will be on the right track. The following actions serve as guidelines to help to strengthen our family and friend relationships:

- listening;
- reaching out;
- not trying to "fix it;"
- reminiscing;
- asking them about themselves: "How are you doing?"
- not saying "me too;"
- respecting, not judging, the experience of others;
- welcoming silence which gives you time to think before you speak and gives them time to mull over their ideas;
- making mistakes and forgiving yourself;
- maintaining confidentiality;
- setting appropriate boundaries;
- getting help when needed; and, most important,
- welcoming the reality of another human being.

The best advice may come from grief specialist Harold Ivan Smith (2006), who said, "The greatest gift we can give to someone is the hospitality to their reality (n.p.)."

Chapter 17

Summing Up

I am hopeful that this book enlarges your view of the subject of grief, and helps you to experience your own power and to appreciate what all of us will go through or are going through.

It all comes down to the universality of this experience of grief. It is love. Even the pain? The shock? The anger? The sadness? The guilt? The lostness and meaninglessness? Yes, it is all contained in love. It is all part of the human design. It is very important and has the capability to uplift us, change us, and yes, unite us. When you go through your own individual grief process and when you come to the point where you can move on easefully in your life, you may not recognize that you are an inspiration to others in their own lives. This has been my experience, and I'd like you to know that your inner journey has an effect on others in your community. In my work, I provided bereavement support to newly widowed spouses. I would be uplifted by their courage. I would be intrigued by their search for meaning. I would be inspired by their ability to just put one foot in front of the other and live their lives.

The aloneness of grief makes grief hard. Even if you are in the same family, each of you will grieve differently. You are alone because you are unique. Yet, at the same time, you are not alone because we are all together.

Many years ago, after my mother died, I wasn't sure how I would make it. I remember driving down the street and noticing people in their cars and walking on the sidewalks. Many of them looked like they were of the age that probably their mothers had died, but they were driving along, walking along, and participating in life. If they could do it, I would, too. I had no idea who they were, but they inspired me to turn the corner and move through life with a little more cheerfulness and lightheartedness.

None of those people knew I was watching them and noticing them. In that very alone moment for me, we were all together. May it be so for you!

"We're all in this together alone."

Bibliography

Alexander, E. (2015, May 5). After her husband's sudden death, Elizabeth Alexander writes their love story. *PBS NewsHour*. Retrieved from pbs.org/newshour/show/elizabeth-alexander-remembers-husband-new-memoir.

Allen, W. (1975). *Without feathers*. NY: Random House.

Anderson, R. (1970). *I never sang for my father*. New York: Dramatist Play Service, Inc.

Bailey, E. T. (2010). *The sound of a wild snail eating*. Chapel Hill, NC: Algonquin Books.

Ball, E. (2015, November). Retracing slavery's trail of tears. *Smithsonian Magazine*. Retrieved from www.smithsonianmag/history/slavery-trail-of-tears- 180956968/.

Baugher, B. (2013). *A guide for the bereaved survivor*. Toronto, Ont: Caring People Press—Caversham Booksellers.

Beck, A. T., & Alford, B. (2009). *Depression: Causes and treatment*, 2nd edition. Philadelphia, PA: Univ. of Pennsylvania Press.

Bekoff, M. (2007). *The emotional lives of animals*. Novato, CA: New World Library.

Bennett, A. (2012). *The cost of hope*. NY: Random House.

Bloomfield, H., Colgrove, M., & McWillians, P. (2000). *How to survive the loss of a love*. Algonac, MI: Mary Books/Prelude Press.

Boaz, J. (2014, June 3). June is PTSD Awareness Month and millions are affected. Letter to the editor. *Penobscot Pay Pilot Newspaper.* Retrieved from the Internet, https://www.penbaypilot.com/article/letter-editor-june-ptsd-awareness-month-and-millions-are-affected/34657.

Bonanno, G. (2004, January). Loss, trauma and human resilience: Have we underestimated the human capacity to thrive after extremely aversive events? *American Psychologist* 59(1): 20-28.

Bonanno, G. (2009). *The other side of sadness.* NY: Basic Books.

Boss, P. (1999). *Ambiguous loss.* Cambridge, MA: Harvard University Press.

Bowers, D. (2006, April 18). *The new normal and the grief process: How the threat of terrorisim has changed us, challenged us, and added the dimension of fear to the grief process.* Paper presented at Widowed Persons Outreach Conference, Washington, DC.

Bowlby, J. (1982). *Attachment and loss, Vol. 1, 2nd edition.* New York: Basic Books.

Buchwald, A. (1994) *Leaving home.* Thorndike, ME: Thorndike Press..

Cameron, J. (1992). *The artist's way.* New York: Jeremy P. Tarcher/Putnam.

Campbell, J., with Moyers, B. (1987). *The power of myth.* New York: Doubleday.

Case, N. (2013, September). I couldn't really listen to music. *Morning Edition, National Public Radio.* http://www.npr.org/2013/09/03/217189246/neko-case-i-couldnt-really-listen-to-music.

Chittister, J. (2003). *Listen with the heart: Sacred moments in everyday life.* Lanham, Maryland: Sheed and Ward.

Coffin, W. S. (2004). William Sloane Coffin's eulogy for Alex. Retrieved March 19, 2020 from http://www.pbs.org/now/society/eulogy.html.

Crootof, C. (1969). Poetry therapy for psychoneurotics in a mental health center. In J. Leedy (Ed.), *Poetry therapy: The use of poetry in the treatment of emotional disorders* (pp. 38-51). Philadelphia, PA: J. B. Lippincott Co.

Didion, J. (2005). *The year of magical thinking.* NY: Alfred Knopf.

Doka, K.J., & Martin, T. (2010). *Grieving beyond gender: Understanding the ways men and women mourn.* London: Routledge.

Duggan, D. R. (2014). *Men, grief and solitude.* Alexandria, VA: Solitude Publishers.

Duncan, R. (Ed.). (2005). *Gandhi: Selected writings.* Mineola, NY: Dover.

Enriquez, J. (2015, October 9). Are we evolving into a different species? TED radio hour: How it all began. Retrieved March 19, 2020 from www.npr.org/programs/ted-radio-hour/357837221/how-it-all-began.

Epstein, M. (2013). *The trauma of everyday life.* NY: Penguin Books.

Fillmore, C. (1969, November 13). A sure remedy. *Unity Magazine.* Retrieved from truthunity.net/tracts/Charles-Fillmore-a-sure-remedy.

Fischer, N. (2005, Spring). Saved from freezing: The spirituality of art. *Tricycle Magazine.* Retrieved from http://www.tricycle.com/feature/saved-freezing.

Frankl, V. (1984). *Man's search for meaning.* NY: Washington Square Press.

Gawande, A. (2014). *Being mortal.* New York: Henry Holt and Co.

Gaylin, W. (1979). *Feelings: Our vital signs.* NY: Harper & Row.

Gelberman, J. H., & Kobak, D. (1969). The psalms as psychological and allegorical poems. In J. Leedy (Ed.), *The use of poetry in the treatment of emotional disorders* (pp. 133-141). Philadelphia, PA: J.B. Lippincott Company.

Gilbert, K. R. (2002, April). Taking a narrative approach to grief research. *Death Studies* 26(3): 223-239.

Gilbert, K.R. (1996). We've had the same loss, why don't we have the same grief? *Death Studies* 20(3): 269-283.

Goldbloom, R. (2017, October 12). The vital things that make life spectacular. *PBS NewsHour, Brief but Spectacular.* Retrieved from pbs.org/newshour/show/vital-things-make-life-spectacular.

Golden, T. (2000). *Swallowed by a snake.* Gaithersburg, MD, GH Publishing LLC.

Golden, T. (2013). *The way men heal.* Gaithersburg, MD: GH Publishing LLC.

Goss, R. E., & Klass, D. (1997). Tibetan Buddhism and the resolution of grief: The Bardo-Thodol for the dying and the grieving. *Death Studies* 21(4): 377-395.

Grollman, E. A. (1995). *Living when a loved one has died.* Boston: Beacon Press.

Hartling, L., Rosen, W., Walker, M., & Jordan, J. V. (2000). Shame and humiliation: From isolation to relational transformation. Wellesley, MA: Wellesley Centers for Women's Work in Progress Publications.

Houston, J. (1988) *Possible human, possible world: Part 1* http://www.intuition.org/txt/houston1.htm, *Thinking allowed: Conversations on the leading edge of knowledge and discovery with Dr. Jeffrey Mishlove* [television series episode]. Retrieved from http://www.williamjames.com/transcripts/houston1.htm.

Jordan, J. (2015, November 20). *Grief after suicide: A training for mental health professionals.* Workshop presented for Jewish Social Services, Rockville, MD.

Jordan, J. (2016, September 16). *Traumatic Loss: New understandings, new directions.* Workshop presented for Jewish Social Services, Rockville, MD.

King, B. (July 2013). When animals mourn. *Scientific American* 309(1): 63-67.

Kübler-Ross, E. (1969). *On death and dying. NY:* Scribner.

Kurlansky, M. (2017). *Havanna: A subtropical delirium. NY:* Bloomsbury.

Lewis, C. S. (1983). *A grief observed.* NY: Bantam.

Lewis, H. B. (1971). *Shame and guilt in neurosis.* Madison, CT: International Universities..

McNees, P. (1996). *Dying: A book of comfort.* NY: Doubleday Direct.

McWilliams, P. (1995). *You can't afford the luxury of a negative thought.* Los Angeles, CA: Prelude Press.

May, G. (1992, Summer). For they shall be comforted. *Shalem News* 16(2): 3.

May, R. (1969). *Love and will.* NY: W. W. Norton.

Mayo Clinic Staff. (2017, September 27). Depression and anxiety: Exercise eases symptoms. Retrieved from www.mayoclinic.org/diseases-conditions/depression/in-depth/depression-and-exercise/art-20046495.

Miller, Richard C. (2015). *The iRest Program for Healing PTSD*. Oakland, CA: New Harbinger Publication.

National Center for Chronic Disease Prevention amd Health Promotion, Division of Population Health. (n.d.). Tips for better sleep. *Centers for Disease Control*. Retrieved March 20, 2020 from cdc.gov/Sleep/About Sleep/Sleep_Hygiene/html.

National Geographic. (2009). Dia de los muertos. Retrieved March 18, 2020 from http://education.nationalgeographic.org/media/dia-de-los-muertos/.

Neimeyer, R. A. (Ed.). (2012). *Techniques of grief therapy*. London: Routledge.

Nguyen, L. (2009, September 18). Life and death the Vietnamese way. http://www.aslantedview.com/life-and-death-the-vietnamese-way/.

Nhat Hanh, Thich. (Producer). (2014, February 11). *Tale of Kieu* [audio podcast]. Retrieved from *http://tnhaudio.org/*.

Nuland, S. B. (1994). *How we die*. NY: Alfred A. Knopf.

Oates, J. C. (2013, June 10 & 17). After Black Rock. *New Yorker Magazine* LXXXIX(17): 96-97.

Ochberg, F. (1993). Post-traumatic therapy. In J. P. Wilson & B. Raphael (Eds.), *International handbook of traumatic stress symptoms* (pp. 773-784). NY: Plenum Press.

Olds, J., Schwartz, R., & Webster, H. (1996). *Overcoming loneliness in everyday life*. NY: Carol Publishing Company.

Palano, H. (2009). *The Talmud: Selections* (pp. 287-299). Retrieved from www.sacred-texts.com/jud/pol/pol37.htm.

Parkes, C. M. (1971, April). Psycho-social transitions: A field for study. *Social Science and Medicine* 5(2): 101-115.

Parkes, C. M., & Prigerson, H. (2010). *Bereavement: Studies of grief in adult life, 4th edition*. London: Routledge.

Pennebaker, J. W., Kiecolt-Glaser, J. K., & Glaser, R. (1988, April). Disclosures of traumas and immune function: Health implications for psychotherapy. *Journal of Consulting and Clinical Psychology* 56(2): 239-245.

Perry, H. L. (1993). Mourning and funeral customs of African Americans. In D. P. Irish, K. F. Lundquist, & V. J. Nelson (Eds.), *Ethnic variations in dying, death and grief: Diversity in universality* (51-64). Philadelphia: Taylor Francis.

Polley, S. (Producer). (2012). *Stories we tell* [motion picture]. Montreal: National Film Board of Canada.

Rando, T. A. (1991). *Grieving: How to go on living when someone you love dies.* New York: Bantam.

Rando, T. A. (1993). *Treatment of complicated mourning.* Champaign, IL: Research Press.

Rando, T. A. (2015). *Core strategies for treating traumatic bereavement.* Presentation for J & K Seminars, Wyncote, PA.

Reiter, S. (2004, December). In Memoriam Jack J. Leedy. *Journal of Poetry Therapy* 17(4): 231-238.

Rosenblatt, P. C. (1983). *Bitter, bitter tears: Nineteenth-century diarists and twentieth-century grief theories.* Minneapolis, MN: University of Minnesota Press.

Rosenblatt, P. C. (1996). Grief that does not end. In P. Silverman, D. Klass, & S. L. Nickman (Eds.), *Continuing bonds.* Washington, DC.: Taylor and Francis.

Rosenblatt, P. C. (2008). Grief across cultures: A review and research agenda. In M. Stroebe, R. O. Hansson, H. Schut, & W. Stroebe (Eds.), *Handbook on bereavement research and practice* (pp. 207-222). Washington, DC.: American Psychological Association.

Rynearson, E. K. (2001). *Retelling violent death.* Philadelphia, PA: Brunner Routledge..

Rynearson, E. K. (2010). The clergy, the clinician, and the narrative of violent death. *Pastoral Psychology* 59: 179-189.

Schaef, A.W. (1995). *Native wisdom for white minds.* NY: One World.

Schoen, M. (2014). *Your survival instinct is killing you.* NY: Plume.

Sheets, H. M. (November 2, 2016). Mark Rothko's Dark Palette illuminated. *New York Times.*

Silverman, P. R. (1969). The widow to widow program: An experiment in preventive intervention. *Mental Hygiene* 53(3): 333-337.

Silverman, P. R. (1996). What's the problem? In P. R. Silverman, D. Klass, & S. Nickman (Eds.). *Continuing bonds* (pp. 3-23). Washington, DC.: Taylor and Francis.

Silverman, P. R. (2004). *Widow to widow—How the bereaved help one another.* NY: Brunner-Routledge.

Smith, H. I. (2006). *Red letter days.* Presentation at Workshop about Holidays and Anniversaries, Widowed Persons Outreach, Washington, DC.

Smith, H. I. (2007). *ABC's of healthy grieving.* Notre Dame, IN: Ave Maria Press.

Stadter, M. (2012). *Presence and the present.* Lanham, MD: Jason Aronson.

Staudacher, C. (1991). *Men and grief.* Oakland, CA: New Harbinger Publications.

Strand, C. (2010, Spring). Turn out the lights. *Tricycle Magazine.* http://www.tricycle.com/feature/turn-out-lights.

Strand, C. (2015). *Waking up to the dark: Ancient wisdom for a sleepless age.* NY: Spiegle and Grau.

Stroebe, M., Schut, H., & Stroebe, W. (2005). Attachment in coping with bereavement: A theoretical integration. *Review of General Psychology* 9(1): 48-66.

Sveen, C.-A., & Walby, F. A. (2008, February). Suicide Survivors' mental health and grief reactions: A systematic review of controlled studies. *Suicide and Life-Threatening Behavior* 38 (1): 13–29.

Swedlund, A.C. (2010). *Shadows in the valley: A cultural history of illness, death, and loss in New England, 1840 -1916.* Amherst: University of Massachusetts Press.

Tangney, J. T., & Dearing, R. L. (2002). *Shame and guilt*. NY: Guilford Press.

Taylor, S. E. (2002). *The tending instinct*. NY: Times Books.

Tolle, E. (2009). *Guardians of being: Teachings from our dogs and cats*. Novato, CA: New World Library.

Weisman, A. (1972). *On dying and denying*. NY: Behavioral Publications, Inc.

Westberg, G. E. (2011). *Good grief, 50th anniversary edition*. Minneapolis, MN: Fortress Press.

Widdershoven, G. A.M. (1993). The story of life: Hermeneutic perspectives on the relationship between narrative and life history. In R. Josselon, & A. Lieblich (Eds.), *The narrative study of lives, Volume 1* (pp. 1-20). Thousand Oaks, CA: Sage Publication.

Williams, D. R., & Sternthal, M. J. (2007, May 21). Spirituality, religion, and health: Evidence and research directions. *Medical Journal of Australia* 186(10): 47-50.

Wolfelt, A. (1988). *Death and grief: A guide for clergy*. Muncie, IN: Accelerated Development, Inc.

Worden, J. W. (2009). *Grief counseling and grief therapy*. NY: Springer.

Worden, J. W. (2015). Theoretical perspectives on loss and grief. In J. M. Stillion & T. Attig (Eds.), *Death, dying and bereavement: Contemporary perspectives, institutions, and practices* (pp. 91-103). NY: Springer.

Yeagley, Larry. (1984). *Grief recovery*.

Select MSI Books

Health & Fitness

108 Yoga and Self-Care Practices for Busy Mommas (Gentile)

Girl, You Got This! (Renz)

Living Well with Chronic Illness (Charnas)

Survival of the Caregiver (Snyder)

The Optimistic Food Addict (Fisanick)

Psychology & Philosophy

Anger Anonymous: The Big Book on Anger Addiction (Ortman)

Anxiety Anonymous: The Big Book on Anxiety Addiction (Ortman)

Awesome Couple Communication (Pickett)

Depression Anonymous: The Big Book on Depression Addiction (Ortman)

El Poder de lo Transpersonal (Ustman)

Harnessing the Power of Grief (Potter)

How to Live from Your Heart (Hucknall)

Noah's New Puppy (Rive with Henderson) [PTSD]

Road Map to Power (Husain & Husain)

The Marriage Whisperer: How to Improve Your Relationship Overnight (Pickett)

The Rose and the Sword: How to Balance Your Feminine and Masculine Energies (Bach & Hucknall)

The Seven Wisdoms of Life (Tubali)

Understanding the Analyst: Socionics in Everyday Life (Quinelle)

Understanding the Critic: Socionics in Everyday Life (Quinelle)

Understanding the Entrepreneur: Socionics in Everyday Life (Quinelle)

Understanding the People around You: An Introduction to Socionics (Filatova)

Understanding the Seeker: Socionics in Everyday Life (Quinelle)

Self-Help Books

100 Tips and Tools for Managing Chronic Illness (Charnas)

A Woman's Guide to Self-Nurturing (Romer)

Creative Aging: A Baby Boomer's Guide to Successful Living (Vassiliadis & Romer)

Divorced! Survival Techniques for Singles over Forty (Romer)

Helping the Disabled Veteran (Romer)

How to Get Happy and Stay That Way: Practical Techniques for Putting Joy into Your Life (Romer)

How to Live from Your Heart (Hucknall) (Book of the Year Finalist)

Life after Losing a Child (Young & Romer)

Publishing for Smarties: Finding a Publisher (Ham)

Recovering from Domestic Violence, Abuse, and Stalking (Romer)

RV Oopsies (MacDonald)

The Widower's Guide to a New Life (Romer) (Book of the Year Finalist)

Widow: A Survival Guide for the First Year (Romer)

Widow: How to Survive (and Thrive!) in Your 2d, 3d, and 4th Years (Romer)

www.ingramcontent.com/pod-product-compliance
Lightning Source LLC
Chambersburg PA
CBHW061302110426
42742CB00012BA/2023